Serious Business

Non-political Humorous Stories to get you through 2020

By Doug Rough

©Copyright 2019

ISBN- 9781687249357

Introduction

This book is a collection of true stories from my life. OK, mostly true. Most are humorous, and I hope all are interesting. None are political. I tried to keep them short and entertaining. I told many of these as bedtime stories to my kids. This book was written so my kids they will have a copy of the stories I used to tell, but I hope my friends and relatives will want to read them, too. Anyone is welcome to read them. My motivation to write this was the recent story *DWTS Saves My Life*. My stories were very nearly lost.

If you decide to use these as bedtime stories, you might want to skip a few the stories, like *Huey's Mom* and *Mansion Photos*, for example. I have marked the ones to not use as bedtime stories and put them at the end of the book in case you want to tear out the pages so children will not read them. Or, you can buy my "Bedtime Stories Only" version. Some of those stories are pretty interesting, though.

Each story is intended to be stand-alone, although if you skip around you might get confused. This is not a read-in-one-sitting book. This is a read-a-few-stories-at-a-time book, like when you are doing some kind of a temporary sitting activity. If you don't use it for bedtime stories, use it for *Serious Business* (that is, as a bathroom book).

Being photographers we have taken millions of photographs. I could have easily filled this book with photos, but I tried to only include a very few illustrative photos.

You are welcome.

Circle or highlight the stories you like best, and re-read those. You are likely to enjoy it more if you stop frequently.

My daughter Tessa's favorites are marked [TF].

My cousin Rick is known to skim all "family letters" for his name, and then only read the parts where his name appears. So I put his name in a few places so maybe he'll read this book. Or parts of it.

I was going to erase the twelve least entertaining stories. Since I had already typed them up and all, rather than erase them I instead just marked them [Cousin Rick].

So, read no more than ten stories a day. Mark your favorites. Cross out (or delete) the ones *you* think are lame. If you have a great story yourself, give me a call at 425-821-5529. This is a land line, so no texting (See *Land Lines*).

If you like this book, please tell your friends to buy it. Or give a few as gifts with your favorite stories already highlighted. Thanks in advance!

Table of Contents

BEFORE I WAS BORN

Walker Bates—When telling stories from over a hundred years ago—especially when these stories get verbally handed down without written anything—there may be, shall we say, embellishments. With that in mind, here is the story as I was told it, of Bainbridge Bates, my father's father's mother's father. Rather than "Bainbridge" folks called him "Walker."

He was born and grew up in Vermont in the mid-1800s. When Civil War broke out, he volunteered for the Army and they put him in the "14th Vermont" whatever that means. He walked to Pennsylvania, where he eventually fought and was injured in the Battle of Gettysburg, wherein he helped repel "Pickett's Charge" near the "copse of trees." What is a "copse" anyway? He says he briefly saw General Lee after the main battle crossing the river.

After spending a month in the hospital, he lost 40 pounds. He was fortunate that he was not wounded in the leg, as many folks left military hospitals with fewer legs than they entered with.

He never talked about this battle until he was over 60 years old. He said it was horrible, unimaginably horrible. It seems that many soldiers died at Gettysburg, but few died quickly.

When he recovered, he walked back to Vermont. On his way, he bought a single plate, one fork and a spoon at Tiffany's in New York City as a gift. (I, too, would be thinking lightweight if I were to buy a gift while walking from Pennsylvania to Vermont).

After returning to Vermont at the age of 19, he farmed for three years and hated plowing all the rocks. He heard about homesteading in Iowa where the farming was easier. You guessed it—he walked to Iowa. There may have been an Ohio River boat ride in there somewhere. When he got there after many months, they were done with homesteading in Iowa, but they helpfully told him they were now homesteading in Nebraska. So, he walked to Nebraska and homesteaded there. Union veterans paid $5/acre. He eventually bought about 400 acres. My dad's cousin Betty still owns most of that farm in Nehawka, Nebraska about 150 years later. Lorraine and I stayed on this farm on our honeymoon.

I wonder why they called him "Walker"?

College for Her Kids— My father's father's father's mother died in childbirth in Lafayette, Indiana. When his father remarried, he didn't get along with his new stepmother, so was sent to live with his father's sister in Nehawka, Nebraska. Stepmothers have that effect on some people. When he arrived in the tiny town where his aunt lived, he saw Francis, an eleven-year-old girl and decided that he was going to marry her when she got older. In a small town back then, I guess this was not creepy at all. They waited seven years to get married, when the bride turned 18 (and the groom was 27). The bride, the daughter of *Walker Bates*, had only a fourth-grade education. All her life she wished she could have gone to school longer. She wished she was as smart as a fifth-grader.

She agreed to get married on one condition: That her children go to college.

All five of her children, one boy and four girls, went to college. Back then, a girl going to college was unusual. Four sisters going was downright weird. One of my grandparents was her son, Stuart. He married Carolyn Shurtleff, a college graduate, and both of my grandparents on my mother's side, William and Gertrude Wilson Houghton, were college graduates, too. Weird.

Walker Bates sitting in front. My father's father's father James Rough in back next to his wife Francis (Walker Bates' daughter) in the dark dress. This was taken in the 1920s. The photographer clearly did not know any good jokes.

Many Relations—My mother's sister Bib provided me a list of

genealogy for my mother's side. I found that my mother's side traces back to the US in the Mayflower days. Because the population was so low, inevitably there were times that cousins married. This means that people like Richard Platt, born in what is now the US in 1604, is my eleventh generation grandfather five times in five different ways.

I guess that means his grandchildren liked each other. A lot.

Bib?—My mother's youngest sister's name was Louise, but everyone

called her Bibber or Bib all her life, because at the time she was born her sister Joan could not pronounce "Baby" very well. It is cute when babies mispronounce *some* words.

Mayflower?

—My mother's sister Bib's genealogy has my mother's family traced to the Mayflower, but there is some Mayflower society that disputes that claim. One thing about genealogy that is clear is that much of the time the data is wrong. My own marriage certificate is wrong—it says we were married in Whatcom County. Not so. I found a book saying my wife Lorraine's grandfather was born in New Zealand and another that claims he was born in the US, but he told me himself before he died that he was born in Norway. Yes, before he died. Plus, people 200 years ago didn't know how to spell their own names most of the time. Some random clerk could "change" the spelling of their name and they would not know. And we all know that fathers are not always fathers, if you catch my drift.

If the chance of an error in each generation is this high, then the chance of an error-free data lineage to the Mayflower is pretty close to zero. So if someone says you are not descendent from the Mayflower, just realize that the data they use to determine that is almost certainly wrong. So there. Didn't want to be in your dumb society anyway.

Surviving a Snowstorm

—In 1888 there was a snowstorm in Nebraska that killed many people. Blizzard and whiteout conditions covered roads suddenly. Many people who were caught on the roads away from home died. Walker Bates (see above) was miles from home in a horse-drawn buggy when the blizzard started. He couldn't see, and even if he could see, so much snow covered the road that he didn't know where the road was. And no walking for Walker, either. Getting home by buggy from where he was involved several turns.

He decided to let go of the reigns. It worked. The horse knew the way home, including all the proper turns. Didn't even need to chain up.

His horse saved his life. The horse likely enjoyed not having the reigns bugging him during the trip, too.

Horses Save Another Life—My great grandfather James Rough was also saved by horses. He was plowing his fields one day and his plow horses stopped at a certain point and refused to go further, so he turned them around each time they stopped, which effectively meant he only plowed about 2/3 of his field.

Later, he heard that bandits had robbed and killed someone who had gone past the point where his horses had stopped. James didn't die or get robbed, but his crop yield was down by 1/3 that year.

Sandy Dunbar—This was my father's father's father's father's father's mother's father. I think. Anyhow, he lived in Scotland in the 1700s. I was told he owned some rather large vats and shepherds would bring him their wool. He would put the wool into the vats of boiling dye and dye the wool all sorts of colors. He was known as a Dyer.

On the last day of his life, he fell into one of his vats, and "died."

Get it? The Dyer died? Nevermind.

Pioneer Grandmother—My aunt Bib told me the story of a relative of ours in the late 1600s before the US was the US and the area was a British colony. This relative, some kind of great-grandmother to me on my mom's side, came home one day from working in the fields and found that local natives had killed her husband and kidnapped her infant son. After reporting it to the British officials, she was told there was not enough local military strength to do much about it, and her son was likely going to be raised as a native. She waited a few days, snuck out at night, took back her son and killed those who had kidnapped him.

Don't mess with a pioneer woman.

Shocking—William Shurtleff, a tenth generation great grandfather (way back) on my father's side was born in England, and showed up in Boston in 1634 at the age of 12 without being listed as a passenger on any ship—I wonder if that was a game of hide-and-go-seek that went awry or if he did that on purpose. He was killed at age 42 by lightning. He was inside his house at the time. I wonder if it was covered by his homeowner's insurance.

War at 16—Ichabod Shurtleff and Rufus Kempton were both buncha-great grandfathers on my father's side. Both were in the American Revolutionary War at the age of 16. Rufus was a drummer. They really did have a drummer and someone playing the flute or piccolo for the soldiers back in the day. And parents really did name their sons "Ichabod."

Sir William Johnson—I am told that Sir William Johnson was a direct relative. We think. Back when the area we now call New York was a British colony, some of the "Indian Nations" had appointed ambassadors, and Sir William Johnson was the British ambassador to the Iroquois Nation, which included Mohawk, Oneida, Onondaga, Cayuga, and Seneca tribes. He had a Mohawk housemaid he renamed "Caroline." Caroline had a son, whom Sir William sent to college, gave him his last name, and generally treated him as his son. I don't know if gossip had been invented back then, but I bet the neighbors had their opinions. We are descendants of Caroline's son anyway. That makes me about 2% Mohawk. I tell people I got the haircut backward.

Five People, Three Names—I found a photo of my father, his sister, brother and their parents when the children were all teens. I call it five people, three names. My father's father was Stuart Rough, as was his oldest son. My father's mother was Carolyn Rough, as was her daughter (later Dunlap). My father (right rear) had the only unique name in the photo. However, James Rough was also his grandfather's name. (Years later, James had a son named James, Carolyn had a daughter named Carolyn, but Stuart blew the whole scheme by naming his son "John" for some crazy reason.)

Five People, Three Names. Two Stuart Roughs, two Carolyn Roughs and a James Rough.

The Name "Rough" –My father and his sister Carolyn both told me that all of my ancestors with the last name "Rough" came from Scotland. Both also told me that our ancestors were poor. Dirt poor. Don't look for a "Rough" coat of arms, they told me, because if you find one it could not possibly be from our branch of the family.

Aunt Carolyn did most of the genealogical research, but it was my father who told the story of golf courses in Scotland. Hundreds of years ago in Scotland there was no private land, and no parks. All land was owned by someone. Anyone who wanted to fish in a stream either owned the stream, got permission from the owner, or trespassed. My ancestors trespassed. They discovered, my father says, that if one kept very quiet, one could fish along side golf courses and not be bothered, particularly if you returned a few errant balls to golfers once in a while. They did this so often and it worked so well, they felt as though they belonged on the edges of golf courses. My father claims that this is the reason the edges of golf courses came to be known as "the Rough."

That is my story and I am sticking to it.

Found a Rough—My father's father's father's father had six sons. His oldest son, the one I was descended from, was by his first wife who died in childbirth. My aunt Carolyn was curious about genealogy and wondered if there were other people named "Rough" that were distant half-cousins from this line. She traced five brothers from the second wife and four of them had no sons. One had one son, who had one son, who had one son. She wanted to invite this person to our next Rough Family Reunion. She found an address for that last son, Harry Rough, in Indiana—in a prison.

She decided not to invite him.

Grandma's Best Story—My father's mother Carolyn Rough was a teacher. Later, she had Alzheimer's disease for the last 15 years of her life. As a result, she told her best story many times, as she didn't remember that she had just told it. Many, many times.

Years after she retired, a man walked up to her and said, "Mrs. Rough, you were my favorite teacher!"

This, of course, is what every retired teacher loves to hear.

"Why did you like me the best?" she asked.

"You taught me how to play baseball" the man said.

Two Trees in Yellowstone—My father's father Stuart Rough
was a school teacher in Twin Falls, Idaho, and he often had a summer job
in Yellowstone National Park. This was back in the 1930s when the park
had few roads, and the ones it had were dirt. He was driving at night and
missed a curve, and his car got stuck between two trees. Both doors were
held fast, so he had to climb out through the window and over the back
end of the car back to the road. He then hiked back to West Yellowstone
in the dark at night where his family was living for the summer, many
miles away.

When he returned with a tow truck the next day, the daylight revealed
that the two trees actually held the front of the car ten feet off the
ground, and had kept the car from falling off a 100-foot cliff.

Yellow Stone Groceries—My father's mother Carolyn Rough
sometimes went weeks without seeing her husband who worked
summers at Yellowstone National Park. This was the 1930s when the
roads in the national park were poor and travel was tough. She kept a
nugget of gold on a chain around her neck. Whenever she ran out of
money—and this happened fairly often—she would promise the local
grocer she would pay him back later by leaving that gold nugget as
collateral. When her husband got paid, she would pay the grocer and
take back her Yellow Stone.

Uncle Stu at Omaha Beach—My father's brother Stuart Rough

was a naval officer in command of the first boat to Omaha Beach on D-Day. His boat had 2000 rockets, and their job was to "soften up" the German emplacements on the hillside. Unfortunately, the only way to aim the rockets was to aim the boat, and the weather did not cooperate. The ship was thrown around by the surf. His rockets went everywhere except where they wanted them to go. After firing all 2000 rockets, they went back to get more. After reloading 2000 more rockets far offshore, his commanding officer made the probably correct call that firing more rockets would be just as likely to hit friendly forces as enemy forces, and so held them back. His ship took no casualties that day.

Uncle Stu and his ship did the same thing for the invasion of Southern France. This invasion did not get a lot of press as there were almost no Germans to be found, so the soldiers had little resistance. His boat was scheduled to do the same thing for the planned invasion of Japan. Stu and everyone in his boat were pretty sure that they would not survive the invasion of Japan, but they were convinced of the importance of having rockets fired to lead the way. Japan surrendered a few weeks before the planned invasion of Japan, thus probably sparing Stu's life. Stu is a true hero to me, not only willing to die for his country, but nearly certain he would die.

After Japan's surrender, Stu's ship full of rockets near the coast of Japan was sunk rather than sailed back to the US. If you are a WWII collector, you are welcome to look for it. Just look for a sunken ship on the bottom of the Pacific Ocean. It's gray—that might help.

My Father in WWII—My father skipped two grades, and so

graduated from high school at the age of 16 in 1938. He then got a Bachelor's degree in physics, and went on to try for a PhD in physics. By the time he was fully involved in his PhD program, the US was fully involved in WWII. Rather than finish the PhD, he chose to become an officer in the US Navy like his brother Stuart and his sister's husband Tom.

By the end of the war, all three were commissioned officers in the US Navy.

As navy war jobs go during WWII, I claim my dad had the best job. He was on a ship patrolling the north-eastern coast of the US, looking for German war ships. They didn't find any. Then, when V-E day happened, they were the first ship into New York harbor. They got the ticker-tape parade, the whole shebang, even though they saw no action. He got invited to hundreds of parties, where thankful women wanted to hear of his exploits. He thought about going to one of the parties in the building where he was staying, but he wanted to visit his brother Stu in Toledo, Ohio who was courting his future wife Harriet. My father knew of a navy aircraft flying to Toledo that night that had room for him to go along for free. So that was his plan. He got late notice that thunderstorms in Ohio had pushed off the navy flight a few days. OK, at that point, he might as well go to a party in his building, where he met my mom.

On the long list of things to be thankful for: thunderstorms in Ohio in June 1945.

Married Before Judy—My parents were married rather soon after they met in 1945 in "The Little Church Around the Corner" in Manhattan in New York City. There were multiple marriages scheduled in that church most days that year, and the bride in the very next marriage on the same day as my parents was Judy Garland. Practically a bridesmaid.

Tom, Carolyn, Stu, Harriet, Marge (mom), Jim (dad), Carolyn, Stu

Fire Engine—When my brother was about three years old, eight
years before I was born, my parents bought him a toy riding fire engine
for Christmas, the kind a kid can climb in and ride around. The fire engine
came in a box with a picture of it on the side, but it was unassembled. My
father took the parts into his shop to assemble it and left the box. My
mom, not realizing the box was empty, wrapped it. My father assembled
the fire truck, but forgot it in his shop.

Christmas morning, my brother opened an empty box with a picture of a
fire engine on the side.

"Oh, boy!" he exclaimed with delight, climbed in it, and started making
fire engine sounds.

My parents could have saved a bunch of money....

Lorraine's Grandpa Chris—Lorraine's mother's father Stanley
Christenson came from a family that was not afraid to travel. His father,
Emanuel was born near Vestra Karup, Sweden on a farm. He said he
never got enough to eat, so he left home at the ripe old age of 12 to work
for a shipping company. As 12-year-olds do, I guess. He ended up in New
Zealand and liked it. After a few years, he opened a store in Gore, New

Zealand, got married to a Norwegian woman and had seven children there. The children all spoke only English. The parents spoke Norwegian or Swedish only when they didn't want the children to know what they were saying.

After running his store for about 20 years, he decided to move to Arendal, Norway, where his wife's sister lived. Sophia, the oldest daughter was 18 and did not want to go. I can see that. Imagine trying to talk a teenager born and raised in New Zealand (a "Kiwi") into moving to Norway. Nope, said Sophia. So they left Sophia in New Zealand by her request.

On the way to Norway, the ship got hit by a tsunami near the equator, but did not sink. Stanley Christenson was born in Arendal, Norway. Both he and Sophia lived well into their 80s and talked on the phone at least once, but it was expensive.

Stanley never met his sister Sophia.

Stanley was the only actual Norwegian of his siblings. Everyone else was a Kiwi, but all were half Norwegian half Swedish. Figure that out.

When little Stanley was only a few months old, Emanuel took his wife and the seven remaining children on a ship to Canada, took a train across Canada and then settled on the north shore of Lake Campbell, Washington (just south of Anacortes).

Emanuel died of a stubbed toe! It got badly infected.

Circumnavigated the world countless times, then finally settles down to die of a stubbed toe.

Later, Stanley worked for Standard Oil Company for 41 years, including opening up the first gas station on the Eastside in Bothell, WA on the corner of Bothell Way and the Bothell-Everett Highway. During the depression he was one of the few people with a job. He met his wife Ruby Sunde because she was waiting for a bus in front of the gas station and he thought she was cute. Ruby's parents, the Sundes, had purchased their property from Captain and Mrs. Beardslee. Their property included the entire area from what is now the Bothell post office to what is now the University of Washington Bothell campus, almost exactly bisected by the road now called Beardslee Blvd.

Stanley is a big reason why I doubt genealogical records. I have one book that says he was born in New Zealand and another that says he was born in the US, but he told me himself he was born in Arnedal, Norway (which matches what a third book says).

If you want to read a different story about *Lorraine's Grandpa Chris*, I have two other books for you.

EARLY YEARS

Miscarriages—My older sister is seven years older than I am because my mother had three straight miscarriages. That makes me my mother's fourth straight miscarriage.

Sparky Saves My Life—When I was newborn, my 11-year old brother wanted me to sleep with him. However, at the time he was sleeping in the top bunk and we had hardwood floors. My parents first said no, but he persisted. When they finally said yes, the first night he rolled over and I went off the edge, and landed square on our collie, Sparky. I was fine, but Sparky barked A LOT.

I nearly died #1.

Day Care at Two—My earliest memory is of going to a new day care. I remember the two steps leading to the house to be huge. I had to climb them but they were normal steps to everyone else. My mom told me that it was just before I was two years old. My mom led me into what looked like a living room with toys spread around. As I passed by a curtain covering a passageway into another room, I started for it. The nice lady told me not to look behind the curtain and showed me all the toys in the living room and asked me to play with those toys. The second she turned her back, I ran over to look behind the curtain. I remember expecting to see better toys and lots of fun things, but I only saw a big pile of dirty laundry. I was disappointed.

The one thing I took away from that story all my life is that whatever you tell a two-year-old not to do, that is the first thing they will do once you turn your back.

The Big Word—[TF] When I was about four years old, there was a kid on our street a few houses down who was my age and he bragged one day that he was so smart he could spell any word. No way, I said. Oh, yeah? Said the kid, tell me the biggest word you can think of and I'll spell it. I thought and thought. "Mountain" was the biggest word I could think of. "M-O-U-N-T-A-I-N" he said. I ran off to my house.

M-O-U-N-T-A-I-N, M-O-U-N-T-A-I-N, I kept repeating in my head as I ran.

When I got home, out of breath, I ran from room to room to find my mom. Finally I found her. "Mom, mom, is this how you spell mountain, M-O-U-N-T-A-I-N?" I asked her.

"Yes." She said.

"Oh" I said, disappointed that the kid was correct.

Teddy Bear—[TF] When I was four years old, I had a Teddy Bear that I slept with every night and kept on my bed during the day. The kid next door who was two years older than me had heard about my Teddy Bear from another kid and asked to see it. I went and got it off my bed. He grabbed it and ran off laughing. I started to cry and ran after him. He ran to the school at the end of our street. He threw the bear up on the school roof. It caught on a sloped part of the roof. It was stuck, but you could see it. I was crying. I said I was going to "tell on him." He said don't worry, he'll get it back. He grabbed my hand and led me back to his house, where he got a ladder. He carried the ladder back down to the school.

The bear was gone.

I cried and cried.

The kid gave me another Teddy Bear, different color, different brand.

Just not the same.

Two Bathrooms—When visitors needed to use the facilities in our house, my mom would tell them "We have a bathroom down the hall or you can go behind the piano."

Family Letters—My mom used to type a family letter every week. This was before the internet, of course, when stamps were 4 cents and long distance phone calls approached $1 per minute. Her family was in Connecticut and my father's family was mainly in California. She would use a typewriter, and use "carbon copies" where what she wrote on the first page appeared slightly fainter on the second page, fainter still on page three, and very faint on the fourth page. I think she mailed the first three copies to her two sisters and her parents in Connecticut and the fourth copy to California.

My cousin Rick was famous in the family for scanning these letters for his name and then only reading the part that had his name in it. (Hi Rick!).

ELEMENTARY SCHOOL AND JUNIOR HIGH

Second Day of School—My mom walked me to kindergarten the first day to get all signed up properly. I wanted her to walk me again the second day but she didn't. I was depressed about having to walk alone and so had my head down and was just watching my feet. I ran into a pole at school and fell down. I sat there rubbing my head and crying for about two minutes, trying to decide whether to go back home or continue to kindergarten.

I had to talk myself into it, but I did eventually go to kindergarten that day. Almost a kindergarten dropout.

First Thing I Learned in School—The first thing I learned in school was that no matter what anybody did to you, boys should not cry. The other boys made sure I learned that lesson.

I was a crier. That was a tough lesson for me to learn.

Serious Business—[TF] In my family, for some reason, my parents said "serious business" when other families said #2 or poop. Of course I didn't know that other people used different words. I had no reason to think we were unusual as the topic did not come up when I talked with other kids.

In first grade, some kid made a joke and most of the kids laughed when we were supposed to be taking a test. Imagine my surprise when the teacher held up a copy of the test and sternly announced that "This is serious business!"

I laughed and laughed. Nobody else thought it was funny. Ahem.

Measles in First Grade—My mom was one of those who didn't think you were really sick if you could walk. One day when I was in first grade, I didn't feel well, but my mom sent me to school anyway. I felt a bit ill all day, but stuck it out. About twenty minutes before the end of school, the teacher looked at me funny. You have spots all over your face! She sent me home. Turned out I had measles. I was gone for a week, and when I returned half the class was out sick and we had a substitute teacher.

Typhoid Doug.

JFK's Death— My first grade teacher was a no-nonsense, tow-the-line instructor. Everyone in that class learned to behave. I was in first grade when an announcement came over the loudspeaker that JFK had been shot and killed. Our no-nonsense teacher burst into tears and ran out of the room.

Nobody moved. We waited, without saying a word. After about ten minutes of silence, the recess bell rang. Slowly, the class got up to go outside for recess. When we got back from recess, we had a substitute teacher. When our normal teacher returned days later, she did not mention the incident.

Three-Wall Caterpillars—[TF] In one class in elementary school there was a contest to see who could read the most books. A paper plate with the book name on it was stapled to the wall in a line for each kid. Artwork was added so it looked somewhat like a caterpillar. I was competing with another boy to have the longest paper plate caterpillar. Our caterpillars ended up going around the room taking three walls. No one else's finished the first wall.

Thirsty—My parents liked to go for "Sunday drives" and just drive around for hours. July 4, 1965 was a Sunday and it was very hot. So we drove around in the heat for a couple of hours, then went to a party we had been invited to. I was eight years old. We had no air conditioning in our car, so I was very thirsty when we arrived. I was first out of the car and ran into the house looking for something to drink. I saw a big punch bowl and glasses. I grabbed the biggest glass, filled it and drained it. Whew! I was better. For a few minutes. Soon, I was bumping into walls. I decided to lie down. I woke up at home.

The punch was spiked! The only time I ever passed out drunk I was eight.

Sparky and Bowling—[TF] When I was about eleven, I walked to a bowling alley about two miles away with a couple of friends. This was back when you never took dogs inside stores, so my dog Sparky walked with us, but stayed outside. When we were done, we walked back home.

The next day, we could not find Sparky. This was very unusual for him. He was never leashed, but he was always good at coming when you called. We called and called, and he didn't come.

Someone asked me which door we used when we left the bowling alley. I realized that we had entered through the front door and left through the side door.

Sure enough, we went back to the bowling alley and there was Sparky patiently waiting at the front door for us to come out.

Wendell's Hot Rock—[TF] When I was in Boy Scouts, we had various characters. One of those characters was a guy named Wendell. Wendell liked to brag. One day the troop had gone on a hike, set up camp and made dinner. After dinner we decided to go on a short hike as there was still some light left before sunset. Wendell told us he was going to have a toasty warm sleeping bag when he got back, because he had taken two sticks and fished out a very hot rock from the dinner fire and put it into his sleeping bag. The whole hike he bragged about how toasty warm his sleeping bag was going to be when he got back.

After we got back from the hike, we looked into his tent. You could see a gooey plastic-covered rock surrounded by about two inches of dirt, then a gooey circle of plastic around that. The rock was so hot that it melted the plastic of the sleeping bag to the plastic of the tent. It was impossible to get into the bag any more, as there was a large section melted to the tent, not to mention the large hole. Those of us who had gotten annoyed with the bragging had the best laughs.

Breakfast Fire—[TF] We had various characters in my boy scout

troop, as I mentioned. I cannot remember who did the breakfast fire fiasco, but it was not Wendell. I'll say "Wendell" anyway just for convenience. Anyway, at a week-long Boy Scout camp one scout was assigned each day to wake up before everyone else and build the breakfast fire. "Wendell" decided to build the biggest breakfast fire of all. When we awoke his morning, we were greeted with a six-foot tall pile of dry cedar logs burning. Cedar, as you may know, burns hotter than most wood. A six-foot tall dry cedar fire is not something you can comfortably stand near. We were worried about our tents 20 feet away. "Wendell" was proud of himself. He had two eggs in a flimsy Boy Scout aluminum pan ready to cook, but the fire was too hot for his hands when he tried to get the pan close enough to cook the eggs. His solution was the proverbial ten-foot pole. He lashed the handle of the pan to the end of a ten-foot pole. This allowed him to be able to push the eggs into the hottest part of the fire without burning his hands. However, the pan disappeared. When he pulled the pole back he had just a couple of inches of handle on the end followed by dripping molten aluminum.

We ended up having to wait a good hour for that fire to die down enough for us to cook breakfast. Good thing, as it took us about that long to stop laughing.

Penelope's Preference—One day I was in the kitchen and I heard what I thought was a cat fight in the distance. A few days earlier there had been a cat fight at our neighbor's house and it sounded like that. I called my sister and she listened, too. No, it sounded different than a cat fight, but it was definitely a far-off cat sound. We opened the back door and discovered that the sound was not outside. Hmmm. We listened more carefully and then my sister thought to open the dishwasher. The head of our cat Penelope popped out from under the bottom rack and let out a series of very loud yelps.

 It took us about 30 minutes of Penelope yelping loudly to extract Penelope from the dishwasher because the only way we could do it was to push her head back in (under water), then pull the bottom rack out and get her out over the back of the bottom rack. Penelope, not recognizing the physics of all that, was not the slightest bit interested in having her head pushed back underwater so we could get the rack pulled out. Both my sister and I had to thickly cover our hands and arms because Penelope scratched furiously at anyone trying to push her head back under water for some reason.

Looking for Nothing—After Penelope, we got a cat we named "Nothing." When that cat got lost, we had to ask the neighbors to please look for Nothing.

Hide and Sleep—[TF] Two friends came over to play one day and my sister Deb and I played hide and seek with them. We could not find

Deb. We called and called. She didn't come out. So, the three of us decided to watch TV. We watched a one-hour show, and when it was done, we got up, and sleepy Deb crawled out from under the sofa where she had been asleep for the past hour.

Visiting Mars—My mom liked to visit older folks who were living alone and drag my sister Deb and I along when we were in elementary school. I thought it was mostly boring, but I know now that this was probably a great highlight for many of these folks. People in their 80s rarely get to interact with elementary school kids. My favorite of all the people we visited was Mar. That was her name, and we liked telling friends we were going to Mars (Mar's). One visit, Mar told me that she had a cake in the fridge and I could have as much as I wanted. In general, I loved cake, and here was a chance to do something (eat cake!) that was more fun than what we usually did, which was try to find something to watch on her tiny black and white TV. She said I could have a big piece and since no one was watching when I dished up, I served myself a particularly big piece. It was bad. I spat it out and threw away my big piece. Later, Mar asked me if I liked the cake. I admitted that I did not. She said "Wasn't that awful cake? I have been trying to get rid of it for two days. I may have to throw it out."

Jack's Toss—During summer evenings when I was about 12, I did what most kids my age did—I went outside. Often in the summer it would stay light until well after 9 pm, and we would stay out and play with the other kids on our street until dark. We would play hide-and-seek, kick the can, capture the flag or some other game, or just toss or kick a ball around. I was lucky that my dead-end street had so many kids, and the number would swell if someone had some friends overnight.

This was one such night, where I saw a group of about 20 kids, and only half of them actually lived on the street. The group had gathered at the beginning of our dead-end street that was next to a fairly busy street. I wondered what was going on. The kids were behind a hedge, about 12 feet tall, that blocked the view of the busy street. One kid was pulling off tiny pine-cone shaped things (okay, I am no botanist) from the hedges, and tossing them over the hedge to land on the cars going by. It sounded like hail hitting the cars. There was a discussion going on as to whether or not this was a good idea. The kid kept tossing. There was another kid named Jack who found a rock about the size of a softball and picked it up. Someone suggested Jack toss the rock over the hedge, but immediately several kids noted that Jack did not seem very strong. Someone stated as though it was a fact that Jack was not capable of throwing the rock high enough to clear the hedge. Oh, yeah? Said Jack, and threw the rock, easily clearing the hedge. Eyes widened as everyone realized that was a mistake. Seconds later: WHAM! The rock hit a car! Glancing around the hedge, I saw a sedan with a dented roof, and a very understandably upset driver climbing out who looked about 25 years old.

Twenty kids scattered in twenty different directions. The driver caught the youngest kid, about eight years old. I could hear him bawling that he didn't do it and didn't know who did. I am pretty sure he was telling the truth as I knew the kid was not Jack and doubted he knew Jack.

That is all I know. I got out of there as fast as I could.

Sparky Skids—We loved Sparky, our collie when I was a kid. Sparky was always fun to play with. One thing we discovered we could do with Sparky was to play chase with him. He loved to chase us. Our kitchen had linoleum, and the rest of the house had wall-to-wall carpet. If you opened our back door about 1/3 of the way open and you exited without moving the door from the dining room, it required running on carpet then taking at least one step on the linoleum. We used this as kids to get Sparky all riled up, get him to chase us, then run out the back door. When Sparky would try to follow, he would hit the linoleum, and skid into the kitchen cupboards with a bang. He was no worse for the wear, always ready to do it again, and we thought it was hilarious.

We only did that when mom was not around for some reason.

Not Fighting with Chuck—[TF] I had a friend named Chuck who

was on my soccer team as well as in my fourth grade class. I don't know how it all got started, but we liked to pretend to fight. We got pretty good at it, too, timing the sound of the punch just right with the fist that barely missed the chin. From a distance, it looked and sounded as though we were having a big fistfight, but no punches landed. I guess we did it because there were always new "recess moms" patrolling the playground and it was fun to see them panic. When they inevitably ran over to us, we would throw our arms around each other's shoulders, smile and say, "What?"

Reddy the Neighbor's Dog—When I was about nine, the next-

door neighbors had a Setter named "Reddy." The dog seemed nice enough, quiet and calm. Our dog Sparky got along with him and the two dogs did not bark at one another. The one thing that annoyed me about Reddy is that he would occasionally poop in our yard. This was back in the days when we didn't even own a leash, and our Sparky was a big collie dog. It only recently occurred to me that I owe our old neighbors an apology for wherever Sparky was pooping, because it was not in our yard.

One Friday in late November, the weather was so nice that we left our back door open. Our back door led into our dining room on one side and our kitchen on the other. I looked out the back window and I saw Reddy leaping over our back fence with one jump, carrying our leftover Thanksgiving turkey in his mouth.

Fisher's—About two miles from my house was Fisher's Drugs, which sold comic books, candy, toys, music and magazines: the five most important things to a kid. Heaven. I walked there a lot, always with a friend or two.

Four of my many trips to Fisher's were memorable.

1. It was a couple of days after Christmas, and I ran into a kid I knew from school in Fisher's. He was really excited to show me something. He had just come back from the Wigwam store next door where he had exchanged a pair of pants he had gotten for Christmas for a "switchblade knife." He said that real switchblades were illegal, but this was a close as you could get legally. He showed me a partially opened folding knife and flipped it to try and open it. He couldn't get it to flip open. After about five tries he flipped especially hard and it finally opened, but the blade stuck into his thigh about an inch. He started to bleed on his pants, which now had a big hole in them. Maybe that exchange wasn't such a good idea….

2. I was a coin collector at the time, collecting old pennies. The woman in front of me had 100 old pennies she dumped out to pay for something. I saw three steel pennies (all steel pennies are from 1943) in the pile and offered to buy those three for three regular pennies. She said fine. All the way home I was kicking myself for not giving her a dollar to buy all 100 pennies and then going through all of them later to look for other old ones.

3. A friend of mine wanted me to go to Fisher's. I loved to go, so that was not a problem, but he was hurrying me as if it was important. When we got there, he didn't want to buy anything. That was annoying because he had bugged me to go. I bought something as I always did. Walking home, he pulled a bunch of stuff he had stolen out of his pocket. He told me it is easier to shoplift if you go through the register behind someone actually buying something. I was pretty mad and never went to Fisher's with him again.

4. It was the first and only time I took the four-mile round trip with my friend Kelley to Fisher's. He was out of shape and seemed to have some foot issues. Anyway, he was going very slowly. What was a brisk walk for all of my other friends Kelley called a "Death march." He had to stop and rest every few steps. I got annoyed. He kept saying, "You're killing me!" and after a while I started to agree. He then started saying "I'd be better off dead!" and I started to agree with that, too. He then said "My feet are killing me!" and I said "I wish they would hurry up!" We laughed for half an hour. It was funnier when I was eleven years old, I think.

Coin Collecting—I was a coin collector when I was a kid. I collected pennies. At one point, I had every penny from 1899 through 1970 except the very rare 1909 S-VDB in a nice book designed to display front and back of the pennies.

When I was in college, someone broke into our house and stole my penny collection. My nice display book was ripped up in the yard.

Small consolation: That thief had gotten about $1 value out of my penny collection worth probably over $200 at the time, because he spent those pennies as pennies.

Lin's Prom—My sister Lin is seven years older than I am. She went to Senior Prom in high school when I was ten years old. On Prom day, she tried to do too many things. She talked to friends, went to the store, got her hair done, baked cookies and got herself all dolled up so that she looked great when her date picked her up. But she forgot about her cookies. They were little charred briquettes. When her date arrived, her helpful brother immediately offered him some of "Lin's cookies."

Swim Team—I was on the swim team for several summers. Practices were before the pool opened to the public starting at 7:30 with public swimming at 9 am. Since none of my friends were awake in the summer at 9:15 am when I got home, I would go back to bed.

The swim meets were divided up into Under Evens (U8, U10, U12, U14) so every other year I got blue ribbons for winning races, and the other years I stunk.

Pete's Home Run—When I was eleven, we had a guy named Pete on my baseball team. Pete was a good hitter, except that Pete swung at every pitch. If the other team figured this out, they could easily strike out Pete. I remember one day the coach telling Pete not to swing at every pitch, but to wait for a pitch over the plate. Pete nodded, as he always did. The first pitch was WAY over Pete's head. Pete got up on his tippy toes and took a big swing at it. He hit a home run. When he got back to the dugout, I remember the coach going up to Pete to talk to him. When the coach got there, they looked at each other and nobody said anything. The coach then looked up at the sky. I am pretty sure he sighed.

Baseball Championship—[TF] When I was twelve years old, my baseball team won the Bellevue city championship. Baseball-wise, it was all downhill for me after that, but at least one of the kids on my team ended up playing briefly for the majors I am told. In the final game, we were ahead by one run in the final inning. There was one out, and there was a runner (from the other team) on third base. I was playing third base, and I was playing ahead of the base next to the runner who was leading off as we thought the other team might bunt. The batter did not bunt. The batter hit a screaming line drive right at my face. I threw my head and myself backwards to keep the ball from hitting me in the face. I barely got my glove in front of my face in time. The ball in my glove hit my forehead. I fell backwards. My butt and back landed on the base, which knocked the wind out of me and the ball up in the air. I had enough presence of mind to realize that I should not let the ball hit the ground. I leaned way over to catch the ball again that had squirted out of my glove before it hit the ground. Somehow, I managed to lean way out and catch the ball again with one butt cheek on the base, just before the runner slid into me trying to get back. I felt stupid as I had tripped and fallen awkwardly and had failed trying to keep the ball from hitting my face more than I was trying to make a play. The local newspaper, however, was kind: "Doug Rough made an unassisted double-play to end the game."

Bellevue Championship "Hawks." I am back middle. I think Pete (see *Pete's Home Run*) is second from left front. Sighing coach is the one on the right.

Canadian Exchange—The best part about playing Seattle-area
youth soccer is the Canadian exchange at the end of the season. Each

Seattle-area team is paired with a Vancouver-area team, and the coaches pair the players. The team drives up to Canada, and each US player is hosted by a Canadian player for the night, then the teams play a game the next day and go home. The next week the Canadian team goes to the US for a similar hosting and game.

Every year we were hosted by a different team. Three exchanges stick out in my memory. One year, the kid who was hosting me lived near a long pier in North Vancouver. We walked from his house to the pier. For some reason, this kid liked to race. He raced me to the end of the pier. I won. We raced back. He won. He then challenged me to race running *backwards*. I am not sure who won, because I stopped well before the end of the pier, but he didn't. He fell off the pier.

He was not injured, but this was November in Canada. The water was not warm. Several people helped fish him out, and then we walked back to his house. The next week he did not come down to the US because I was told he had pneumonia.

The second memorable exchange was with a kid whose family owned a five-pin bowling alley. He was pretty good at it. It was the one and only time I have ever played (or seen!) five-pin bowling.

The third memorable exchange was when I was hosting two kids. Sometimes the teams did not match up exactly and so occasionally somebody hosted two kids. The three of us were telling ghost stories and stories about peeping toms—people who would look into your window at night and do nasty things to the folks they saw inside.

It got very late, and my mom came in and said the three of us should be sleeping. We said we could not get to sleep. What have you been talking about? She asked. We told her. She walked over and pulled the curtains shut. We fell asleep right away after that.

Years later, when I was coaching the Chargers girls team, I inquired about the Canadian exchange program and was told it was for boys' teams only because there were so few girls' teams. Heck with that. I called around, found a girls' team in Canada and set up an exchange for the Chargers. I am pretty sure the Chargers were the first girls' team to have a Canadian exchange.

Arguing—The Rough family, meaning mostly my dad, his brother Stu, his sister Carolyn and their parents all liked to argue. My mom (as well as Stu's wife Harriet I am told) would calmly leave the room.

My brother said the only person his college roommate ever got in an argument with was my dad. My brother and dad argued a lot.

I think one of the reasons I liked soccer so much is that my dad knew nothing about it, so he had difficulty arguing with me about it.

Once, Carolyn actually claimed that the dictionary was wrong. Winning an argument with a Rough was not possible.

I once started to tell a story to Carolyn by saying, "You know how the Roughs like to argue..." to which she interrupted, "No they don't." Honest.

Like my mom, I would try and leave the room, usually.

In high school the debate team coach told me that he would love to have me on the team as I seemed to be a debate natural. I was horrified that he saw that trait in me since I hate arguing.

My brother ended up being a collaborative facilitator, about as far away from arguing as a profession gets.

I found out late in life that my father had been on jury duty three times in his life. In each of those three times, he hung the jury eleven to one. Did not surprise me a bit.

Dodgeball—In sixth grade, a new PE instructor at my elementary school taught my entire sixth grade class how to play dodgeball. After we learned the game, the school principal decided that the game was too dangerous, and suddenly there was a no dodgeball rule. Our class had just learned the game, and we liked it. The entire class went out and played dodgeball at recess in spite of the new rule. The entire class then had to sit and write "I will not play dodgeball" 25 times each, less than a week after the school had taught us the game in PE class.

Mark's Firework—My good friend Mark was always interested in chemistry. He ended up getting advanced degrees in chemistry, but in fifth grade, he just liked it. One day he announced that he had made a firework, all by himself. He had drilled out a piece of wood and filled it with chemicals. He gathered four friends, and explained how after he lit it, we would see first red flames, then green, then silver, then gold, then several colors at once. He was very excited. He put it out in the dirt field near the school.

When he lit it, the four of us—no dummies—ran behind the school. Boom! Mark's firework blew up and left an eight-inch deep hole. I don't understand, Mark said.

I don't think he ever got over the fact that it was exactly what his four friends expected.

Dad's Minute-Man Model—My father worked for the Boeing company for almost 40 years. Most of the time he was working for the military side of Boeing, as opposed to the side that made the commercial airliners that many folks are familiar with. The military side designed military planes, along with missiles and rockets, etc. Although he was not allowed to talk about the military projects he was working on, sometimes it was obvious, even to a grade-school kid like me. One time, he had designed a "Minute-Man Missile" whatever that was, and he was supposed to deliver the model to someone at the Pentagon in Washington, DC. To make sure that he didn't misplace it somewhere, the model was in a case that was handcuffed to his wrist. We took him to the airport that way.

I remember thinking that was the dumbest thing I could think of—hey spies! Here is the guy with the model you want. Just look for the guy handcuffed to a case.

My Aunt's Chocolates —One summer we flew back east to see my aunt (my mother's sister) and stayed at her house. Soon, I got the flu. I felt awful. I didn't want to go to a restaurant for lunch with everyone else. Since I was about twelve, they thought I could stay home alone in the living room until they returned. I did so. On the coffee table in the living room was a two-level box of fancy dark chocolate candies. While I waited for them to return, I ate that entire box. Then I threw it all up.

To this day, I cannot eat fancy dark chocolates, but the plain stuff is fine.

Piano Lessons—I took seven years of piano lessons. Hated every minute of it. Every minute. Seriously. When I was finally allowed to quit, I told my parents—again—that I had hated it. My parents told me "Someday you'll be glad you had piano lessons."

I am over 60 years old and I am not glad yet. Maybe next year.

Sofa Jumping—[TF] My sister Deb and I were jumping on the sofa one day. We knew we were not supposed to do that. We often forgot that our sofa was pushed up against a curtain, and behind the curtain was a sliding glass door no one ever used.

In time to one of our jumps, the slider shattered. Deb and I got down off the sofa and looked at each other—we knew we were in big trouble. Then my dad came storming in. We braced ourselves.

"Is everyone alright? I was practicing golf in the back yard and accidently broke the slider."

Whew!

Christmas 1970—1970 was the worst year of the "Boeing Bust" when Boeing laid off a huge percentage of its workforce in Seattle. This was when the famous billboard was put up saying "Will the last person leaving Seattle please turn out the lights?" My father was one of the lucky ones who did not lose his job. Many neighbors lost their Boeing jobs, including the father of Randy, the kid who lived a couple of doors down from me. Although Randy's father lost his job at Boeing, he quickly got another job at the local gas station. Being 14 years old, I did not realize the implications of this. I found out at Christmas time.

Christmas 1970 I remember getting a new bike, a watch, several games, new soccer shoes, new clothes, etc. That was just the bigger stuff, there was plenty more. My three siblings were similarly blessed. Our family gift was a new color TV, quite a bit larger than our previous TV. When I saw Randy on Christmas day, before I mentioned my haul I first asked him what he got for Christmas that year. He asked me to follow him into his house. There, in the living room was a new color TV. He pointed to it proudly. I admired it even thought it was not as nice as ours. What else? I asked.

That was it. Like me, Randy had three siblings. That year, Randy's entire family got one gift, the TV. That was it for Christmas in their household.

Randy then asked me what I got. I changed the subject. My stomach hurt. The Boeing bust had just punched me in the gut.

Patrol—When I was in sixth grade, I was a "patrol" which meant that I held a stop sign flag in crosswalks so kids could cross the street to go to school. All patrol got to go to the amusement park at the end of the school year for free. This included unlimited rides, plus a hot dog and a drink.

After the patrol group had spent the morning doing rides, we all ate our hot dog and drink together. A kid named Randy (not my neighbor) had not gone on any rides because he was afraid. For some reason, this was unacceptable to the other kids. They insisted Randy go on at least one ride. Randy resisted. Finally, they talked Randy into going on the Ferris Wheel, which was thought to be the tamest ride at the park. When Randy got to the very top of the Ferris Wheel, he barfed his hot dog and drink, which landed smack on the ride attendant. Ewww, said the attendant, who ran off to wash up, leaving Randy at the top, crying, for about 15 minutes.

Poor Randy not only hated the one ride he went on, he didn't even get to keep his hot dog and drink!

50-foot fall—We had tall fir trees in my backyard growing up. I thought nothing of climbing a 150-foot fir tree, usually about half-way up. One day when I was about 13 I was out in the woods near my elementary school and I climbed a fir tree. As I got about 50 feet up, I realized that I could see far better than usual. I had a very clear view. Then, snap! The branch I was standing on snapped. Snap! The branch I was holding onto snapped. I realized that the reason I could see so far is that there were no needles. The tree was dead and so were the branches. I fell stomach first and broke dead branches with my stomach all the way down until I got to the last branch, a big fat one which was not dead. That last branch caught me in the stomach such that I did not break any bones when I landed on the ground with the large pile of branches that came with me. However, I could not breathe for about 15 minutes, since about 30 branches had hit me in the stomach.

Moon Landing

Moon Landing—I was twelve years old and totally enamored with everything about the moon landing in the summer of 1969. By the July 20 landing date, I had already watched TV for several days pretty much every waking hour during the countdown, launch, orbit, etc. When the moon landing occurred, I was ecstatic and full of energy. I kept jumping up and down. I could hardly wait for the moon walk, but they announced that the actual moon walk was going to take place at least two hours after the landing, while the astronauts checked lots of "systems." There would be nothing to see for at least two hours. To burn off some of my energy, I suggested to my mom that we go play 15 or 20 minutes of tennis. The two-mile drive to the tennis courts was dead silent—we saw no cars, heard no kids at the nearby parks or schools and heard no cars on the nearby freeway. We only played a few minutes because the total silence was so eerie and unsettling.

We were clearly the only people not glued to our TVs. We went home and glued ourselves back to our TV. Spoiler alert: The mission was a success and everyone came home safely even though the "computers" they used were nerds sitting at desks in Houston.

Looking 70

Looking 70—When I was in first grade, one of the other first grade teachers had gray hair. I knew a few kids in her class. When I was six, I thought she looked about 70 years old.

Thirty years later, some kids from her class organized a reunion and invited her. I was at another event and stumbled upon this reunion somehow. When I was 36, I thought she looked about 70 years old.

HIGH SCHOOL

Radio News Prize—When I was in high school, one of the local radio stations told listeners that the first person to call in a major news tip got a cash prize. One of the kids at my school burned down the school library, then was the first to call the radio station about the high school library burning. He gave his name and address so he could collect the prize.

His call to the radio station was several minutes before the first call to 911 to report the fire. Oops.

Red Card—I refereed elementary school kids playing soccer when I was in high school. In one game, I saw a forward draw his elbow back and smack the defender in the face when he thought I was not looking. It was the first flagrant, nasty foul I had seen refereeing elementary school kids. I showed the kid a red card. In soccer, that means you can no longer play, and normally the team cannot replace you. The kid's coach asked me if he could substitute for the kid who was tossed out. I knew some of the rules were different for kids than for adults, but I was not sure about this one. I said okay, so they replaced the kid.

The father of this kid screamed at me the rest of the game from the sideline. Telling me what a lousy ref I was and how I didn't know the rules (in the case of red cards, he was correct in that the team should not have been allowed to replace his son).

I had walked to the field. The father screamed at me the entire way home, screaming at me as I walked home, and walked up my driveway and didn't stop until I shut my front door in his face.

I was silent during this walk home, but he had a very small head, and the whole way home I was thinking about how tiny his brain was.

Clean Ears—[Cousin Rick] My mother liked to clean her kids' ears with a Q-Tip. She would sit on a stuffed chair and we would lay with our head on her lap with our legs in the air upside down and she would clean away. I greatly enjoyed it, even though it only took a minute or so. Up to age 16 I asked my mom to clean my ears. Do stuffed chairs remind everyone of clean ears or is it just me?

First Solo Flight—We got a call one day that one of our cousins was flying from Portland to Bellevue (yes, Bellevue, WA used to have an airport) on his first solo flight. My family trooped on down to the local small airport to see it. I had never seen a plane land at the smaller airfield before. We waited, and sure enough, we saw the plane approaching. His plane got lower and lower, but didn't seem to quite get to the runway until there was no runway left. His plane kept going right off the end of the runway, across the street, and stopped in a bunch of bushes. No injuries, but plenty of embarrassment.

I found out that day that it is important for planes to land heading INTO the prevailing wind.

Choir—Our church needed male voices in the choir. I said no, as it did not sound like fun to a high school kid like me even though a friend was doing it. My dad offered to pay me $1 per session if I would sing in the choir. OK.

My pay was probably on the higher end of the typical musicians' pay scale.

Thanks—In high school I briefly helped in a Kindergarten class. One memorable moment was during recess one day where a little boy was crying, hanging from some playground bars, maybe three inches from the ground. I gently picked him up and set him on the ground. He immediately stopped crying and calmed down, put his hands in his pockets, and sidled up next to me looking in the same direction as me. In his best five-year-old, man-to-man voice he said simply, "Thanks" and slowly walked away without looking back.

First Time Babysitting—When I was a sophomore in high school I was involved in a lot of sports, coached soccer, was in chess club and got fairly good grades. I was a busy guy. I had lived in the same house all my life, but about two years earlier we got new neighbors directly east of us toward the dead end part of our street. Thanks to the 20-foot hedge between our houses and my busy schedule I rarely saw these neighbors. Meanwhile, my younger sister had quite the good reputation as a babysitter, so she saw many of the people on our street, including our next-door neighbors to the east quite often.

One Saturday I got a call from these neighbors asking for my sister to babysit that day. Last minute, from 2 pm to 7 pm. Could she do it? I told them my sister was not available, sorry. Could I do it, they asked? Hmmm. I had never babysat, but I had a rare open Saturday. Couldn't be that hard, I thought. Okay, I said.

I went next door and was greeted by the parents, and their kids Bobby and Suzie, about ten and six years old. I remember kinda zoning out a bit and looking at the interesting things hanging in the kitchen when the parents were telling me that I had to feed the kids dinner, because they had left out the food and were telling me how to work the oven, even though it was the same oven we had. I got this, I thought.

They then left, and I got out some board games. I played several board games with Bobby and Suzie, easily made them dinner and even dessert, and we were in the middle of another board game when the parents got home at 7 pm. How did it go? They asked. Fine, I said.

Where is Timmy? They asked.

Uh...Timmy...?

Our two-year old? You don't know where our two-year-old is? He was napping in his crib when we left. We looked in the crib. No Timmy. Crap. I was sweating now. Never saw or heard the two-year-old, and Bobby and Suzie didn't mention him. Sure I lived next-door, but I didn't know they had three kids.

The parents started to panic. Calling his name, they frantically looked in unlikely places in the basement.

Just then another neighbor came through the front door carrying a two-year old covered in mud wearing only a diaper. He had been playing in the creek! For five hours.

They paid me, for some reason. No tip, though. Never babysat again until I had kids myself.

Friday Poker—I had a poker game—penny ante—at my house pretty much every Friday night when I was in high school. It was usually the same characters, Mark, Alex, Dan, Mike, Dave, sometimes Bill or Greg. Mark usually won, Dan almost always lost. Big win or loss was $5, which was cheap even then for a night of entertainment if you lost.

After consistently losing all through high school at poker, I was excited to learn that Dan had gone to Las Vegas and won enough to pay for his entire trip plus return home with an extra $80 in his pocket. That made me very happy. I estimated that $80 was about what he lost in all the poker games he attended at my house combined.

Cordless Phone—One night at a poker game somebody needed to make a call on our phone which was attached to the wall in our kitchen. This was in the early 1970s. The handset disconnected somehow from the cord. He pretended to still talk on the handset as he went outside. Everyone laughed and laughed. Nobody could imagine talking to someone outside on a phone without a cord.

Lady Constance—[Cousin Rick] One day Sue asked if she could attend our Friday night poker games. Sure. It was not a "guys only" game—we were just a bunch of nerds who didn't know many girls.

However, Sue didn't play any of the games. She just brought banana crème pies and watched. She started to consistently attend the games, just to watch, and always brought banana crème pies, I think because they were Dave's favorite. Dave called her "Lady Constance."

Based on my limited experience, those who bring banana crème pies to poker games are popular, even if they don't actually play poker.

Tells—In poker, a "tell" is when the player does or says something that signals to the other players what is in their hand. One Friday night we got a friend of my sister Deb to attend our poker game and to play. She did not do too well, due to tells. In her case, she would tell other players what her hand was.

Blow-in Cards—One day I was at Alex's house and he mentioned that he enjoyed reading the many magazines that he subscribed to, but he was annoyed by all the "blow-in" cards. These were cards that the magazines contained when you got them, but they were not attached to anything and would fall out on the floor when the magazine was opened. Almost all of these cards were no postage needed post cards where you were supposed to put your name and address on the card to get "more information" about something or other. Usually some college info. Anyway, Alex had collected these blow-in cards and showed me this deck of what looked like about 100 cards.

We got an idea. We decided that our friend Mark needed "more information." We filled out all the cards with his name and address and mailed them.

Alex and I forgot about this prank. About a year later when we were high school seniors, Alex, Mark and I were discussing college at Mark's house and how we had each decided on our chosen college. Mark seemed amazed that neither Alex nor I had gotten any hand-delivered college material, as he said that at least twice a week someone hand-delivered some college material to him at his doorstep. Mark showed us a stack of college materials in his bedroom at least four feet tall.

Ahem. At that point, we confessed. Mark threw a bunch of college materials at us.

Mark Disappears—My same friend Mark became a chemical
engineer, and got a job working in Qatar for a company that provided housing plus paid a ton of money. Mark became very rich. He had three kids and admitted that he named one of his kids after our daughter Amanda after having met her and being impressed with both her and the name. I would only get together with Mark every five years or so when he came back to the US for a visit.

Mark and family moved briefly to a wealthy suburb of Los Angeles at the insistence of his wife, because she hated Qatar. We visited them in LA, and noted that Mark's nice cars were parked in the driveway. Why? We looked in the large garage, and it was floor to ceiling full of toys. I remember thinking that it was just not possible for three kids to enjoy that many toys, much less access them. We stayed with Mark and his wife, intending to sleep in their spare bedroom, but they insisted that we sleep in the master bedroom because they "never use it." Hmmm. The following year they moved back to Qatar as the money was too good for Mark to pass up.

A few months later I got a call from Mark. He said that his wife had left him, filed for divorce in Los Angeles, and because Mark did not show up for the hearing, she won everything she asked for, which was full custody of all three kids, plus a huge monetary settlement. Mark said he was not going to give her the money, so he was going to change his name and "disappear." He would never talk to any of his friends or family again for fear that his wife's lawyer would be able to track him down. So this was our last conversation. I was stunned. I stayed on the phone for a good hour, going over the good times. Finally, I said good-bye for the last time. A few minutes later, I got a call from Mark's mom. She screamed, "Do you have any way to contact Mark?" She has in hysterics. I never heard from Mark again.

Alex's Dummy—[TF] My friend Alex was frustrated that people going along a particular road tended to go about 50 mph when the speed limit was 25 mph. He decided to do something about it. He rigged up a pulley about 20 feet over the road, and hung a dummy suspended on a fishing line from it. Late one night as someone sped down the road, he quickly pulled the pulley system and the dummy scooted across the road and was hit by the vehicle. The impact snapped the fishing line and the dummy flew into some bushes. Since the dummy was just clothes stuffed inside clothes, the car was unharmed. Alex ran and picked up his dummy and went home the back way. That'll teach that driver not to speed, thought Alex.

About an hour later, Alex saw a couple of police officers on his doorstep. Well, they found me, he thought. I won't lie he promised himself before opening the door. The officers asked him if anyone in his household had been injured in a car accident recently. No, said Alex truthfully. Off they went without another word.

Summer at Ski Areas—Alex liked to hike in the summer (when the snow is gone), in areas that were ski resorts in the winter. One entire wall in his bedroom was a tapestry of tied-together broken ski equipment.

Methylene Blue—Alex discovered that methylene blue—a chemical used in aquariums—is harmless to humans if you drink it, but it turns your pee blue. All of the teenagers Alex could convince (and there were a surprising number of girls) peed blue for a while.

After all, what teenager doesn't want blue pee?

Alex's Pipe Bomb—My friend Alex liked to make home-made gunpowder. One day he talked me into watching him make a pipe bomb stuffed with his gunpowder. I refused to even be in the same room as he was drilling a hole in the side of the metal pipe full of gunpowder for his fuse and screwing on the end cap. I thought these activities might set it off, but they did not. He put in a very, very long fuse. Too long, we later found out. He put the pipe bomb in a hole between the concrete foundation of an underground electrical vault and a steep hillside near a very rarely used road. He thought that would be a place where all blast material would only go upward making it unlikely someone could get hit. He lit the fuse and we ran west about a quarter-mile to a spot where we could watch. The fuse took almost ten minutes.

We waited. We had not seen a vehicle in over an hour. After five minutes or so, we heard the faint sound of a motorcycle coming toward us on the main road. No, don't turn down that side road, we silently pleaded. He did. That motorcycle, the only vehicle we had seen in over an hour, decided to not only go down this rarely used side road, but for some unknown reason decided to cut the corner in such a way that he drove onto the shoulder of the road close to the electrical vault, just as the bomb went off. BOOM! He fell off his motorcycle—appeared uninjured—but he was pissed. He seemed to think some kids had thrown a firecracker at him and was swearing at these imaginary kids in nearby bushes. The real kids were a good ¼ mile away in the other direction. We couldn't hear what he was saying because he was yelling away from us. Normally, we would have laughed at the guy screaming the wrong direction.

We were not laughing.

I am sure glad the guy was okay. I never did anything like that again!

These days something like that might have made national news, and the FBI might have been asked to investigate.

Hot Seat—I was in an advanced Spanish class, and once a week each person in the class had to sit in the seat next to the teacher and answer questions in Spanish. The teacher called that seat the hot seat or silla caliente. Alex, (who else?), actually installed a working burner into a folding chair and gave it to the teacher as the new silla caliente.

Kim Stops the Walk of Shame—When I was in high school, dances were awkward for everyone. Boys would line up on one side of the dance floor and girls would line up on the other. The music was always too loud. Boys would cross the dance floor to ask a girl to dance. Usually, the boy would then be joined by the girl he asked on the dance floor. Sometimes, the boy would return without a dance partner to the boys' side. This was the Walk of Shame. I swear there were boys who only went to dances to laugh at other boys making the Walk of Shame.

Nobody knew why any boy made the Walk of Shame—it was too loud. They just laughed.

Every boy wanted to avoid the Walk of Shame.

I certainly did. I figured the main reason you could get a "no" was that the girl was "going steady" with someone else. I tried to look for clues. There should be a law that girls who are going steady wear something obvious at a dance that tells other boys not to ask them. This law should be retroactive to all high school dances in the 1970s.

I also did not want to ask one of two girls talking together lest I insult the girl I did not ask. I also worried that a girl might say no if she was not in any classes with me. Dances were a mental struggle for me.

Kim was one of the few girls would venture to the boys' side. Maybe she knew I was a nerd who had trouble walking across the dance floor. I don't know if she did this for other boys, too, but she would point out a girl to me and say (shout, as the music was too loud), "Doug, that girl has not danced yet. Ask her to dance." Hooray! An opportunity to avoid all the mental gymnastics and zero chance of a Walk of Shame. Kim said ask her so I would.

Kim made sure every girl danced, and I never had the Walk of Shame. Thanks, Kim!

Ghost Towns—My friend Mike bought a metal detector and he decided that it would be fun to search for old coins in ghost towns. He and I decided to go on a road trip to Eastern Washington ghost towns and see if his metal detector could find some old coins. We had two maps, one from the present (about 1975) and one from about 1890. We looked for good-sized 1890 towns that either didn't exist or appeared to be much smaller in 1975.

We found Adco on the 1890 map, but it was not shown in the later map. We looked carefully where the town was supposed to be, but we only found a queen bed and mattress. No houses, buildings, foundations or coins.

We found Irby in 1975 was a town of population 7, but it was much larger in 1890. In Irby, we found an abandoned two-story schoolhouse. Although signs said no trespassing, we went in to take some photos. Later, we were looking at our maps and planning our next move, and a truck pulled up. A classic, blue overalls farmer complete with hay in his hair and thumbs hooked in his armpits came up to us and said, "I hear tell ya bin in my SCHOOLHOUSE!" I froze. Good thing Mike was glib. He explained that we only took some photos because we thought it looked so nice, and the farmer was satisfied with that.

We found a newspaper dated 1945 in the tiny town of Douglas. We slept in an abandoned gas station where the price was 22 cents per gallon.

After going to Douglas we went to the tiny town of Ruff, and found out the locals pronounce it "roof." We found some residents and told them we were looking for ghost towns. They said, 'The only ghosts we know live in the city."

North Cascades Trip—When I was a junior in high school, I

decided to go camping in the North Cascades National Park with high school buddies Mike, Alex and Dave. We took Mike's 1957 Chevy, and it broke down in the middle of nowhere, a good five miles from the town of Diablo, population maybe 25. The car gauge said it was out of oil, and when we checked the dipstick, it showed zero oil. None of us were particularly smart about cars. Mike and I decided to hitch a ride back to Diablo to buy some oil. When we got back, the car had been torn apart. The back seat was on the side of the road. Mike was not happy. Why was his car torn apart? Dave said that Alex thought he had locked the keys in the trunk and they were trying to break into the trunk. When Mike pulled the only set of keys out of his pocket, Dave called Alex a moron and proceeded to chase him into the woods.

We had to call them back to put the car back together. Then, the car would not turn over. Again, none of us were good with cars, but we thought the battery had died from the car being taken apart. We knew you can start a manual transmission car by putting the car in gear while it is in motion. We used the slope we were on and put the car in gear. The wheels locked up. Uh, oh. We figured out that this meant the engine was likely seized up from driving it without oil. Not good.

We were on a slope, so we coasted the car toward a campground about a half-mile away downhill. Just before the campground, there was a big curve. We almost did not make the curve because the brakes failed due to overuse while coasting. We very nearly went into Diablo Lake.

We found someone at the campground willing to take Dave to get his dad's car, a two-hour drive away. Dave returned in a little over three hours. I am pretty sure speed limits were ignored.

Climber the Dog—[TF] One warm summer day my friend Bill and I were sitting on the grass in his back yard talking. He told me about a dog named "Climber" that he hated. This was very unusual. Bill normally liked all dogs. I asked him why he hated Climber. Bill said that although Climber lived quite a ways away, he would always come into Bill's yard and pee on the house, the car, just about anything, and his mom always made him clean it up. Just then, I saw a dog enter the yard directly behind Bill. I asked Bill what Climber looked like. Bill started to describe Climber, but before I could interrupt him to say something, the dog ran up and peed on Bill's back.

Yep, that was Climber.

One of several times in my life when I laughed so hard my stomach hurt.

Tackle Football with Mongo—There was a kid we called "Mongo" after the guy in Blazing Saddles because he was big, strong and the nicest guy. One summer day when we were in high school we decided to play tackle football in Mongo's backyard. This guy was huge, about six foot four, and he ended up getting a full ride in college as an offensive lineman. There were five on each team, Mongo and the four smallest people, and the other team (my team) had everyone else, including the second largest person, third largest, etc. Mongo's team got the ball, and handed it to him. The five of us tried to tackle Mongo, but he dragged all five of us the length of his backyard for the score. That ended the game, as it was obvious we could not tackle Mongo.

Squirting Fancy Cars—Renton was a town near us where people who had hot rods liked to drive them up and down the "strip." The stoplights were notoriously poorly timed (There are bumper stickers that say "Renton: Un-synchronized light capital of the world"), which was perfect for showing off your fancy car. My car was not fancy, but I had one in high school, and not many of my friends did, so we went down to "the strip" one night. I had six friends in the car, including Mongo, the big, strong loveable football player friend of mine. Unknown to me, someone in my car had brought a large squirt gun, the kind that sprayed a fairly large amount of water. That person sprayed a highly polished hot rod, and the driver took offense. The driver got out of his car, and started to come after me. I was momentarily worried, but then the driver saw Mongo. Like a cartoon, he stopped suddenly as he saw Mongo and his eyes got wide. He then slowly turned back to me and said "Don't do that anymore!" and jumped in his car and sped off.

My Brother Playing Softball—My brother Jim was the quarterback of his high school and college football teams, as well as the captain of both the basketball team and the baseball team. In short, he was a great athlete. I was eleven years younger than he was, and I remember at age seven trying to decide if I wanted to try to catch the bullet pass he had just thrown toward me or should I let it go and run after the football. I was pretty good at catching bullet passes as a seven-year-old.

I was excited when my parents took me to California to see him at Occidental College when I was about nine. I was curious to see where he was living and had missed my big brother. It was between sports, but my brother managed to get on a recreational softball team and we went to see him play. Jim was playing left field when someone hit the ball over his head. This baseball field did not have a fence in the outfield, the grass just got taller. Jim ran back, tracked down that ball and threw it home.

What a throw! You could hear it coming. It sizzled, it whined! It was a perfect strike, about two feet high over the center of the plate, a good fifteen feet ahead of the batter rounding third base.

"Gaaah!" screamed the catcher as he got out of the way. The ball slammed into the base of the backstop with a loud shutter, hitting the backstop before it ever hit the ground. The catcher, obviously worried about getting injured by Jim's throw, made sure that the ricochet didn't hit him either.

Wimp! I was so mad!

Football Tryout—I would have been a good quarterback. I was catching bullet passes at the age of seven and I was pretty accurate in my throws. I practiced with my brother the quarterback of his high school and college teams all the time. When I tried out for the football team as a seventh-grader, there was a line of guys trying out for quarterback throwing to a receiver who was a friend of the guy who was the existing quarterback. My first throw the receiver sped up to make it look as though I had thrown the ball behind him. My second throw he did the opposite to make it look as though I threw in front of him. My third throw I nailed him with a bullet pass as he made his cut—too early, but I slammed him in the numbers to show him I knew what he was doing. The coach was clueless. Next, he said. Then, the coach set up paired blocking drills where one player would try to block the other, then roles would be reversed. I was pre-puberty, and I was paired against a post-puberty ninth grader who had set some league records. It didn't matter who was supposed to be the blocker and who was not, as soon as the whistle blew, I was flat on my back out of breath. I quit football. It was not fun.

A year later, I was at a fair and I came across a booth where you paid $2 and if you threw a football through a tire, you won a prize. I thought there must be a catch as it looked too easy, but I paid my $2 and threw the football through the tire. "First one today!" said the attendant as he gave me a big stuffed animal. I realized then that not everyone was as accurate with a football as I was.

Seeb's Birthday—[TF] My brother Jim had about five good friends who all had the first name James and went by the nickname Jim. As a result, they had to have other names for themselves. They decided to play one of the cleverer pranks I have ever heard on one of the Jims, we'll call him Seeb.

This was in Junior High School. At this particular Junior High School, every Tuesday at the end of the day, one of the library helpers would go to each class and announce who had overdue books. Those who had overdue books had to go to the library to either pay a fine or return the books, and those who did not have overdue books could go home. One of the "Jims" noted that Seeb's birthday would fall on a Tuesday. They decided that Seeb, who rarely checked out books, should have some overdue books. They had to be careful to check out books with exactly the right timing so that he would get notified on his birthday. Carefully planning, the four Jims each checked out books on the correct days such that the books would be overdue on Seeb's birthday. They soon discovered that carrying lots of books around was a giveaway, so they re-shelved the books as soon as they checked them out. By the time the "window of opportunity" was up, the four Jims had checked out a third of the books in the library and re-shelved them. All in Seeb's name. Now they waited.

On the Tuesday of Seeb's birthday, instead of a library helper, the librarian herself—a big battle-axe lady—came into the room and nearly shouted, "Where is Jim S.?" When he was pointed out, the librarian grabbed him by the arm, yanked him totally confused from his seat and marched him off to the library.

Once it was all sorted out, all the Jims were required to put the library back in order. The librarian never did appreciate the humor of the situation.

Charger Fire Drills—When I was in tenth grade, I got a call from a woman I knew from church who asked me if I wanted to coach a kid's soccer team. I had played soccer since third grade and loved it. I was even refereeing a bit at that point. I jumped at the chance: Yes, of course. She asked if I would still coach if the kids were girls. I admit I hesitated. Ok, I said.

Thus began what was a great experience for me as well as for the girls. The team I was assigned to was a bunch of ten- and eleven-year old girls. I was sixteen. At that age, five years is a big gap—I was in high school and they were in elementary school. Later, as adults, five years seems like a very small gap, especially as one of the girls (now women) that I have kept in contact with, Sydney, has a child the same age as my daughter Tessa.

I think I learned as much from the girls as they did from me. We were competing against teams that were being taught by a "RPWNP" or a Reluctant-Parent-Who-Never-Played. The typical RPWNP is not a great coach ("you kids nun around. I need to sit for a while"). I knew defense well and I lucked out and got two girls who were very, very good at scoring. One, Annette, ended up getting an article about her in Sports Illustrated when she was in college because she set some college soccer record. As a result, we usually won pretty easily. That made it fun as we could concentrate on helping the weaker players get better once we led by a couple of goals.

It wasn't easy at the beginning. One of our two best players, Rhonda, at first was a pain. She would interrupt, tease the other girls, and generally make a coach's life tough. We needed her, and we could not afford to keep her out of the game when she acted up. I came up with a system that worked better than I thought possible. A point system, where I gave each player points for trying extra hard, fetching balls that were out of bounds, and for generally being helpful. The player with the most points at the beginning of the next game got to start at the position of their choosing. The next ten players got to start, but at the position of my choice. Once I started that point system, Rhonda had the most points every single week, with no exceptions. She went from being the least to the most helpful player on the team.

I felt as though the girls were not aggressive enough at first when the other team had the ball. I kept trying to get the girls to aggressively go after—or charge—whoever had the ball if the other team had it. We worked on this quite a bit from the earliest practices, as that seemed to me to be the area they needed most work on. After several practices, we decided that the team needed a name. What should we name the team? The girls wanted "Chargers." Why? Because "that is what you are always saying, "Charge her, charge her!"

All of the girls preferred to go with me in my parent's station wagon to the away games. All 14 or so girls would cram into the vehicle, back in the days when seat belts were not required. If we stopped at a red light, all the girls would get out, run around the vehicle in a "Chinese Fire Drill" and get back in before (usually) the light turned green. I didn't start this, but I didn't discourage it either. The girls enjoyed it so much that they all refused to go to away games with their parents, preferring instead to "Chinese Fire Drill" their way to the away games.

Two seasons we got everyone on the team to score at least one goal. It is heartwarming to see the entire team cheer as the only player who had not yet scored a goal scores! The first time we did it, the local newspaper noted it with a strange headline: "Charger Finds Range, Joins Team With Goal."

I made a rule for our team that no one could score more than three goals. Our most prolific scorer, Rhonda, kept coming up against this restriction. I remember one game where Rhonda had already scored three goals, but had dribbled past the goalie, who fell down, and the defense who ran into each other and also fell down. She dribbled up to the goal line and turned to look for a teammate to pass to. No teammates nearby. "Coach!" she screamed at me with her back to the goal. "What am I supposed to do?" she yelled as she calmly back-heeled the ball into the goal a split-second before the goalie, who had gotten back up, jumped at the ball at her feet and missed. The spectators all laughed.

I coached the Chargers for five seasons, ending when I went away to college.

One of those girls, Sydney, is now my dentist.

The Chargers. Alex, Stacy, Kim, Kelly, Sydney, Trish, Patty, Doug; Debbie, Cindy, Rhonda, Tina, Annette, Jayne, Bridgette, Keri. Their record was 11-0 the season this photo was taken. Alex had just put his hat on Debbie, who said, "Get that filthy thing off my head" which is why she is scowling and he is laughing. Played well, bot not well matched: Two different orange jerseys and the coaches wore "last year's red."

Chargers Tournament—I entered the Chargers (the girls soccer team I coached) in a tournament. One problem was that the league the Chargers were in was for sixth grade girls, but the tournament was organized by "Under 13" and "Under 14" etc. If we signed up for Under 13, then our oldest girl, Stephanie (not shown in the photo), could not play. She was not our best player, and not our worst either. She was average, but she was on the team. We decided to enter the tournament as Under 14 (U14) even though we would be one of the youngest teams.

We did well. We won all of our games. In a "single-elimination" tournament, that would have been it. However, this tournament was a "double-elimination" tournament, which meant that we had to play the winner of the loser's bracket, because that team had only lost once and you had to lose twice to be out. One last team to beat, but this team had the most post-puberty girls of any of the teams we played. Besides the obvious physical changes when a girl enters puberty, she also gets stronger, taller and faster. We had only one post-puberty girl (the oldest, the reason we were playing U14), and each of our other players seemed to be about six inches shorter than every player on this team. We had not played them yet, but they had lost to a team we beat, so we were ready.

We thought we were ready. We lost 3-0. In soccer, that is a big loss. We had never lost like that to a girls' team. In practice, I sometimes had the Chargers play against a strong boys' team that always beat them, but this was the first big loss to a girls' team, even if they were older and post-puberty.

But this was double-elimination. Now we had only lost once. The only two teams left had each lost only once, so we had to play again. The first game, the one we lost 3-0, was a full 90-minute game. We had to play a 20-minute "mini-game" to decide the winner of the tournament. They had beaten us because they were stronger and faster, so we made some adjustments. The Chargers won that mini-game 2-0, so we won the tournament. I guess puberty does not increase endurance.

Dorothy Falls Off Her Bike—[TF] I was a high school senior
coaching the Chargers one day when I heard a loud motorcycle enter the road alongside the soccer field. The road was steep, coming from the top of a hill. I saw a fast-moving bicycle dodge the motorcycle, then fall onto the road. The motorcycle drove off, but it was clear that the bicyclist was injured. From the angle I saw her fall, it looked to me as though she hit the road face first. My assistant coach Alex and I ran to her, along with a couple of other bystanders.

When I got there, she was a mess. Her face was torn, her lips sliced, her teeth mostly gone. There was a deep wound in her forehead where I was pretty sure I could see her brain. It was awful. She was screaming, "It hurts!" through lips that flapped blood. I tried to stop the bleeding with whatever I had. Someone took off his shirt and we used that, someone else had a handkerchief and we used that. A white bone was sticking out where a finger should have been. It looked as though most of the damage was to her face, and it was horrible.

What is your name? Someone asked. "Dorothy" she said. Suddenly I recognized the name and voice as that belonging to a beautiful girl from a sophomore class where I was assisting the teacher. I could not believe it, as this was no beautiful girl I was looking at now.

Although the four of us tried to stop the bleeding as best we could until the ambulance arrived, I thought she was going to die, mostly due to the brain injury she appeared to have.

About a month later, Dorothy came up to me in school and thanked me for saving her life. She had lots and lots of stitches on her face, but otherwise she was the same beautiful girl I remembered before the bike accident. I didn't think I saved her life, but I was glad to have helped. I was happy for her. I decided not to tell her I was quite surprised that she was alive, but I was.

My First Date—My first date was in high school with a girl named Cheryl. Not the homeless Cheryl I met years later, but a different Cheryl. Cheryl and I went to dinner, then I wanted to show her a place I knew that had a great view of Seattle. I did not know at the time that this particular spot was known as a "lover's lane" of sorts, I just knew from my running cross country that this place had a good view. I had just gotten back from bible camp, which I had enjoyed a great deal. At bible camp, campers gave each other "warm fuzzies" which were big hugs where you rubbed the back of the person you were hugging. As we stopped to look at the view, I told her about "warm fuzzies" and offered to give her one. We were alone in a deserted area, and suddenly Cheryl got very nervous and wanted to GO HOME, NOW. I realized then that I was making her afraid and nothing I could say or do would calm her down. I took her home and I admit I avoided her for the remainder of my high school days. I was painfully embarrassed.

As an adult, I realize now that if Cheryl's father had seen us parked there, he probably would have yanked me out of the car and tossed me in the bushes. Or worse.

Funny how certain painful memories can affect you for the rest of your life. I vowed then and there that I would never again do or say anything that would make a woman fear me. Cheryl, if you are reading this, I am sorry I made you afraid, but I have tried very hard to keep the vow I made after our date to never make a woman afraid of me again. And thank you.

My Date with Ellen—Ellen was the long-time girlfriend of my good high-school friend Tom. Tom and Ellen were a couple for almost two years, which is forever in high school.

I liked Ellen, but she was Tom's girl. However, when I found out one day that the two of them had "broken up," I thought, what the heck? So I asked Ellen if she would like to see a movie with me. We saw "Monty Python and the Holy Grail" which to this day I think is the funniest movie ever made. I could not stop laughing. I don't know if my laughing was a problem, but Ellen said she wanted to go straight home afterwards, so I took her straight home. (This was my second date and I was two for two on "straight home").

A week later, she and Tom were back together and we never dated again.

About six months later, I was at a party with many friends including both Ellen and Tom and the subject of "Monty Python and the Holy Grail" came up. With a group of friends listening, I asked Ellen if she had ever seen the movie. Her gaze turned icy: "I saw it with you" she said simply.

Oops.

Ellen was an amazing soccer player, easily the best female soccer player in the state. She was the star and Captain of the state championship girls' soccer team in high school. Ellen coached the one girl's team the same age as the Chargers that gave my Chargers team trouble. The Chargers barely beat Ellen's girls' team the one time we played them, 1-0, on a lucky goal. Ellen went to Stanford University before they had a women's soccer team there. She started on the men's team her freshman year. The next year Stanford formed a women's soccer team, and in the very first women's game, Ellen took the kickoff, dribbled through the entire opposing team and scored. That is how good she was.

People rarely knew she had two fake teeth on a dental retainer, but if anyone mentioned to her how beautiful she was, she would pop her retainer out and give them a big missing-two-front-teeth smile. In spite of her self-depreciating humor, Ellen was runner up in a beauty contest once.

I stayed friends with Ellen in spite of my oops on the movie date. She graduated straight As from Stanford without getting so much as an A-, then went on to premed school at the University of Washington. She was with a group of premed students at a large hospital in Seattle specializing in heart disease when she suddenly dropped dead at the age of 24. She had hole in her heart no one knew about and surrounded by doctors at a heart-specialist hospital she could not be saved. That was an awful day for me. Her obituary headline in the Seattle Times said simply "Star Soccer Player Dies."

My Friend Tom—Tom was my best soccer buddy in high school. Tom and I were bench-warmers on our high school team that was expected to take first in state in soccer (ended up 2nd). Newport High School's team had a huge amount of talent (many of the players went on to professional careers and one, Terry Hickey, played for the Seattle Sounders). Tom and I decided that rather than be bench warmers on the winning high school team, we would rather be starters on a not-so-great club team, so that is what we did. Although we missed out on practicing with a lot of great players and having "front row seats" during games, we preferred to play. And we did. We had great fun.

After a couple of seasons the Chargers team I coached got very popular, and I had to split the team up because too many girls signed up. I split off about 15 of the new girls and got Tom and another other two friends of mine, Al and another Doug, to coach the new team, which they decided to call the Hustlers. Even as a new team they did well, as they had good coaches.

Tom decided to go to Alaska for college. This didn't sit well with his long-time high school girlfriend Ellen. They broke up for good. Ellen went to Stanford (see *My Date With Ellen*). Tom also had a stubborn streak. Tom decided that he was not going to ask for financial help from his parents and was going to put himself through school, at least partially because his parents didn't like his choice of going to school in Alaska.

College was expensive, and Tom had three jobs to try and pay for it. As a result he fell behind in his school work. At one point, he was late for some paper, and the professor would not take the paper late. If the paper was late, it did not count and Tom flunked that class. If Tom flunked that class, then he was ineligible for at least one of the jobs he had on campus and ineligible for new loans, which in turn meant he could not pay his rent. Tom's unfortunate solution to all of this was to put a pistol to his head and pull the trigger at the age of 21. Tom died, but only after the coroner estimated nearly an hour of extreme agony. The bullet did not kill him instantly.

I wish I could have talked some sense into Tom. I would love to have him back. He was a great friend. I miss you, Tom.

Not a humorous story, sorry. But the moral is important—suicide hurts, and not just you.

My Third Date—In spite of two consecutive "straight homes" on my first two dates, I tried a third. I took her to a Seattle Sonics game (remember them? They moved to Oklahoma later). Parking is bad in Seattle, but I saw a store that was open only from 9-5 and it was well after 5. The parking lot was empty. I thought they wouldn't mind having a car parked in their empty lot while we watched the game.

They did. We spent more time on this date getting the car from the towing lot than we did watching the game. I was way too embarrassed to call her again.

At least we didn't go straight home.

Me and My Uncle—I was in high school and walking in the local grocery store with my uncle, who was visiting. Some woman I barely knew came up and said to my uncle, "Oh, Mr. Rough, it has been so long since I have seen you! It is great to see you again!"

My uncle did not recognize her. He was "Mr. Rough" but so was my father. My uncle and father look somewhat alike, and we both thought the woman probably mistook my uncle for my father, but we could not be sure.

Skiing with Siblings—The only time I have ever gone snow skiing with all three of my siblings was in high school. It was night skiing and very icy. I skied with my brother and my two sisters skied together on the same run, but elsewhere.

I lost my balance on a particularly icy slope. I started to fall forward and my pole caught in the ice and hit me in the face. I felt something hit me in the mouth, but it didn't hurt as my face was so cold I could not feel anything. I looked at my steel pole and it was bent in half. I looked down at the snow and a big drop of blood fell from my mouth onto the snow.

Uh-oh.

I felt around with my tongue and two of my front teeth had been knocked out and were in my mouth! I started to say something to my brother and didn't even have to finish my sentence as he could see the problem.

We realized we needed to find our sisters and go to the hospital (as it turned out, we went to my dentist). We were wondering what to do next when we saw them on the chair lift.

My brother yelled "Meet us at the lodge. We have to leave right away!"

My sister Lin yelled "Why?"

My brother yelled "Doug knocked his teeth out!"

My sisters' chair was moving this whole time and about to go over a hill. Just before they passed out of sight, we heard Lin yell over her shoulder, "Jim, you LIAR!"

I have to admit, knocking my teeth out while skiing in the middle of a show field was a bit incredible.

But they did meet us at the lodge, and we drove to my dentist who put my teeth back in. Years later, one fell out and I got fitted for a fake front tooth, which I still have.

Brown Ceiling—I learned to drive in my father's car. He drove it to work every day. One Saturday I accidently dropped a can of soda, then picked it up and opened it while getting into the driver's seat. It sprayed everywhere, including on the brown ceiling. I went and got paper towels to clean up. When I cleaned the ceiling, it turned out that the ceiling was not brown. It was actually bright white. My dad's heavy smoking had turned the white ceiling brown.

Jean goes to Mt. Rainier—Before she became my brother Jim's wife, Jean flew to Seattle from upstate New York to meet us. My mom decided to drive everyone to Mount Rainier National Park, about a three-hour drive, chatting the entire way. After about an hour of driving, my mom mentioned how disappointed she was of one of Jim's previous girlfriends, largely because she was so sullen and unexpressive. For example, she didn't "ooh and ahh" when she was taken to Mt. Rainier. Jim did not like talking about previous girlfriends, so he changed the subject, and we started talking about Jean's family.

Two hours later, we pulled into a parking spot near the main visitor center in Mount Rainier National Park. Seconds after stepping out of the car, Jean said, "ooh, ahh!"

Watching Soccer—When I was a senior in high school, I was coaching soccer, refereeing and playing myself. I wasn't dating, because my three tries did not go well. When I could, I would also attend the soccer games my sister Deb played. Although Deb is two years younger than I am, she was one year behind me in school so the girls on her team were juniors. I enjoyed watching Deb's team play.

At half-time one game, Deb told me that one of the girls on her team would say yes if I asked her on a date.

I thought I was watching them. I didn't know they were watching me.

Seattle Sounders—In 1974 I was 17 and playing a lot of soccer. The Seattle Sounders professional soccer team was formed and I went to the very first game right after playing a game myself. The Sounders won. After the game, the friend I went with wanted to go to the player's tunnel and get autographs. I went with him, but was not interested in autographs myself, so I waited, leaning against a wall a few feet over from where several Sounders were signing. Some kid asked for my autograph. I gave it to him. Soon, a line formed....

Hit by a Car—My first day of high school, I tried out for the cross country team. I was already running about seven miles a day, and I wanted to show the team that I could keep up with them. When the coach told the team what route to take, they ran off. I had to get more specific directions, as his cryptic remark to the team did not mean anything to me. As a result, I was several blocks behind the team on the first day, but I wanted to catch up. They were running along a winding road (Coal Creek Parkway), that had a speed limit of 35 mph but most folks went 50 mph or more. I could see the team ahead of me, and they were running straight along the winding road, thus crossing the road several times in order to run the straightest route. I chose to do that as well, to try to catch up. But I ran in front of a car.

The car was speeding as most did, and rather than running back to the right-hand side of the road where I started, I chose to try to run toward the left side of the road to let the car pass to my right. The car tried to go around me to the left, going into the oncoming lane. I then ran into the shoulder on the left side, and the car followed into the shoulder. I was going to try to jump for the embankment, but realized that the car was coming too fast and was going to hit my legs. I didn't want my legs broken, so I did the only thing I could think to do, which was to throw my legs up in the air so the nose of the skidding car did not hit my legs.

It worked. The hood of the car came under me and my butt slid up the hood of the car with my legs high in the air. Up the windshield I went to the top of the windshield. The car was skidding like crazy throwing rocks from the shoulder everywhere. As the car came to a halt, my butt slid down the windshield, down the hood and off the front of the car. (Later, I went back and measured the distance between when the car tires stopped skidding and my feet started skidding: 14 feet.) After I stopped skidding on my heels of my shoes, I sat down, and realized that except for a slight cut on my hand on from the windshield wipers, I was fine. I jumped up and ran to the driver's side window and apologized to the driver for running in front of him. I'll never forget what he said.

"Humbla, humbla, humma, dahh!" was what he said. The driver was as white as a sheet, babbling incoherently and shaking uncontrollably. When he finally started speaking English, he asked me if I needed to go to a hospital. I told him I was fine, but he didn't look so good.

I looked up the road. The team, about ¼ mile ahead of me, was looking back but did not stop. I decided to keep going as well. It was a 10-mile course, and I had only done a half-mile of it.

Nine miles later, as I got within about a half-mile of finishing the course, the coach screeched to a halt in a car next to me as I ran along the road. "Rough! I heard you got hit by a car!"

"Yeah, coach, what about it?" as I kept running.

"You need to have your parents sign those insurance waivers and date them YESTERDAY!"

I nearly died #2.

Hit by a Bike—In my experience getting hit by a bicycle while running was much more painful than getting hit by a car. But that was just me.

I had been on the cross country team at my high school for over a year, and no longer felt the need to run with the team. As a result, I was running a route that involved fewer cars in a neighborhood setting where most drivers went the speed limit of 25 mph. Seemed reasonable. I was running in an area that was a steep downhill. I was about eight feet from the curb running in the parking lane along a wide residential street. There were no parked cars this day. There were no cars at all. I heard the high-pitched whine of a bike behind me. I decided to get over closer to the curb, moving to about three feet from the curb and ran there for a few seconds. I didn't want to run on the grass beside the curb as footing can be slippery on a steep slope, but I kept hearing the bike get closer, I decided to jump up onto the grass on the other side of the curb to let the bike pass. Wham! The bike hit me mid-air and threw me fortunately toward the grass. I skidded on the grass on my knees and elbows for what seemed like fifty yards or so. The bike crashed on the street.

My butt hurt from getting hit by the bike and my knees and elbows were bloody because the grass I skid through had some small rocks and sticks in it, but I didn't appear to have broken any bones. I got up to tell the biker what an idiot he was. He had slid on pavement, which made his scrapes much worse, plus I could see that he had broken his arm and his bike was ruined. I decided he had been punished enough and didn't yell at him.

A car drove by slowly. The driver looked at us, and then drove off. The same car moments later backed up, and the driver this time rolled down his window to look, then drove off again. A third time, the same driver backed up and this time asked, "Are you guys okay?"

"No!" we both said at the same time emphatically.

The driver drove us both home. Unlike the time I got hit by a car, I did not choose to finish my run after getting hit by the bike. I ended up being okay except for the scrapes and a sore butt. The biker with the broken arm said he tried to pass between me and the curb.

Idiot.

I nearly died #3

My Mom Dies—My mother was one to take care of others before she took care of herself. We had the same doctor for the 18 years that we had lived in the same house in the Eastgate area of Bellevue and in all that time my mother had taken her four kids to the doctor many times. But she never once had gone for herself. She hated medicine and preferred to lie down rather than take aspirin for a headache, for example.

In March of 1973, she went to our family doctor for herself for the first time ever. My stomach hurts, she said.

Take a couple of aspirins and call me back if it doesn't get better said the doctor. As if she was a hypochondriac.

She just did more lying down, and did not call back.

Three months later, she went back. I am hurting, she said.

Take a couple of aspirins and call me back if it doesn't get better said the doctor again.

Well, we were going on a three-week driving vacation, so she didn't call back.

On our vacation, my mother's stomach started to swell. She was 51 at the time, but she thought she was pregnant. She went back to the doctor after we got back in July. This time he tested to see if she was pregnant. Nope. He wanted to run some other test, so he asked her to not eat for two days, then take a pill, wait 30 minutes, and drink some fluid he gave her. She got the pill-fluid thing backwards, so he sent her home with instructions to not eat again for 24 more hours, and do it in the right order. The test was negative.

He then took a long needle and took a sample of fluid from her bloated stomach, something he later admitted he should have done first. It tested cancerous, so she was rushed to the hospital for emergency surgery.

She had not eaten in three days.

They found cancer in her uterus, but doctors could not complete the surgery because she was too weak. They closed her up to wait until she "got stronger." She didn't get stronger. She died in December 1973. I was a junior in high school just two weeks past my 17th birthday.

Our family doctor asked us to please sue him for malpractice. My father chose not to.

The day she died, she told me not to go to school the next day or the day after. When I finally felt like going to school, she said, "Just tell them your mother died, and they will understand."

[This is painful. Over 40 years ago and yet I weep as I type this.]

Waking Dad—A few months after my mother died, my father asked my sister and I to make sure he didn't sleep through his alarm before we left for school. Sure enough, at breakfast we heard two alarms in the distance. We went into dad's room and he was sound asleep. We shook him. We removed the covers. We banged pots and pans. We jumped on the bed. Finally, we poured water on his head. Nothing. We went back to breakfast.

He came charging in about ten minutes later, yelling at us about how he had told us to wake him.

We tried, dad. Why do you think you are all wet?

Four-page story—One day in an English class everyone was required to write a four-page fictional story about relationships. Alan, a friend, told me that his story got very complicated, with plot twists and interesting details, and suddenly he realized that his four-page story was over six pages. It was well past his bedtime and he was getting sleepy. It

was due the next morning. He thought it would be at least six more pages the way he was going but he did not have that much time. So, he had all of his main characters walk across a street at the same time and get hit by a bus.

I remember this when I think of the last season of Game of Thrones.

Break-ins—Our house was broken into a couple of times a few years after my mother died, possibly because it was empty during the day. The thief seemed to know how to open a window in the back we had trouble locking. Various things were stolen including my coin collection and my mother's wedding ring. My sister noticed that the junior-high school girlfriend of the kid next door, Bobby, appeared to be wearing my mother's wedding ring. My sister had a detective she knew give Bobby a call. My mother's wedding ring appeared on our doorstep the next day.

Airplane Hangar—When I was in high school, I kept a list of punch-lines in my pocket, so I was always ready to tell a joke. I was too lazy to write out the entire joke. At a family gathering someone found my list, and asked me to tell a few jokes, I did, but I could not remember the joke corresponding to one of my punch-lines: "airplane hangar." They thought this was even funnier than the jokes I had told. Just then, my sister Lin came into the room and asked what we were talking about. Jokes, she was told. Someone then asked, "What do you call someone from Warsaw trying to catch salmon?" My brother said, "airplane hangar!" and everyone laughed, including Lin. Then, as Lin's laughter died down, she suddenly said, "Wait, I don't get it!"

The real answer—a fishing Pole—is not as funny as "airplane hangar" or Lin's admission.

If you know the real airplane hangar joke, please let me know. I still forget. I am sure it is pretty funny.

COLLEGE

Going to College—I decided in high school to go to Whitman College. I thought I might like it, so I got on a bus one day, went there and got a personal tour (from a knockout blonde, which I am sure helped me decide). I applied and was accepted.

Meanwhile, after my mother died, my father turned into an alcoholic. It was pretty bad. He started going through about a half-gallon of whisky per week. He also was not rational when he was drunk. He loved to argue, and drinking made it worse.

My father refused to sign the college papers. Since I was only 17, that was a problem. I met with the Whitman College people and they would not make any exceptions. A parent had to sign. I only had one, and he was drunk almost all the time.

My second choice was Western Washington State College (which became Western Washington University—WWU—my first year there). They allowed my 28-year-old brother to sign the papers for me and I was admitted (and graduated from there after four years).

It turns out students are not required to have a drunk man sign something to attend WWU. Not that I am bitter or anything.

Choosing a Major—I was on a chair lift at a ski area with my brother and I told him I didn't know what my major should be in college.

"What are you good at?" asked my brother.

"Math" I said.

"So major in math" replied my brother.

So I did.

Ultimate Sacrifice—Since I met my wife Lorraine at WWU and I know that my mom would have signed the papers Whitman needed, I know my mom had to die for me to meet Lorraine, as painful as that sounds.

Also, my brother Jim was in the final stages of taking a job in South America in an area that later had political instability and bloodshed. He did not take the job when my mother became ill and ended up staying in the US. It is a good bet my brother ended up happier than he would have been in South America. It is certainly possible he could have been killed in the later conflicts.

My brother and I both almost certainly had better lives due to my mother dying. I think she sacrificed herself.

Mom, thank you for your ultimate sacrifice. Thank you for letting me meet Lorraine. I know that you love Lorraine and my daughters, even though you have never met.

Laundry Learning—I was broke at college, even more so than most, as my father had decided he was not going to pay anything. It was all me with loans and jobs and a $600 scholarship (not huge).

No one had ever taught me how to wash clothes. I was too dumb to ask. I figured it couldn't be too hard. I took some quarters down to the laundry in the basement of the dorm and looked at the machines. I noted that it was the same price for hot water washing as it was for cold water washing. I wanted the best deal, so I washed all of my clothes, nearly all cotton, in hot water with hot rinse.

I shrank all my clothes. I did not have money to buy new clothes, so I became known and the guy who always wore "floodies." Pants that did not reach the ground were called "floodies" in reference to hiking up your pants in a flood. Climate change may bring this style back, but in the 1970s, the *very worst* fashion mistake you could make was to wear pants that did not come within an inch of the ground or touch it.

I had shrunk every pair of pants I owned and when I wore any of them you could *see my socks*! Major turnoff for the girls. And in the four years I was in college, we did not have a single flood! Sigh.

Vacuum Cleaner—One friend moved into a studio apartment in Seattle in a high-rise with a nice view. After he moved his stuff in, he realized he didn't own a vacuum cleaner, and he briefly wondered where he should get one. Later, he decided to look out the window at his view. A vacuum cleaner sailed by from above. He went out to the street and brought it back into his new apartment. It was badly clogged. It took him over an hour to unclog it, but after that it worked fine.

My friend apparently had more patience than his neighbor in the unit above him.

Cookie Monster—The WWU campus cafeteria was all-you-can-eat. They served freshly made cookies, but to try to keep the students from taking too many cookies, each cookie was put on a plate, and you had to take the plate. The idea, I guess, was that your tray would get too heavy with all the plates or something. I am pretty sure I was the only person on campus that was allowed to take the cookie without the plate, since I stacked the plates so high they were afraid they would slide off and break. (I was running eight miles a day at this point, plus playing soccer). I would go up to the area where the woman was putting cookies on plates. When she saw me she would sigh heavily, put two handfuls of cookies on my tray and then tell the next kid he had to take the plate.

Hitchhiker—In college I was broke. One weekend I needed to go to Seattle and thought I might hitchhike. It was only my second time hitchhiking, the first being during my *North Cascades Trip*. It was raining and I got a ride right away. The car looked like it had been in a wreck then fixed up by an amateur. There was a drip from the roof into my lap. The driver said he had something for that drip in the glove compartment. It was a rag to put in my lap.

I asked the driver where he was going, and he said he didn't know. We were headed south, so I suggested Oregon or California. He said he didn't know. I should have stopped there, but I asked him where he was coming from. He said (I swear!) that he had just killed someone and was running from the law. He saw my eyes get wide and he said, "Don't worry, I was drunk. I am sober now."

Not sure why, but I don't hitchhike any more.

John's World Record—John was the guy who lived in the dorm room next to me at WWU. John had lived in the same dorm room for seven years. Seven years! That must be a world record. Anyhow, while I was taking 18 credits per quarter compared to the standard 15, John would start with 12, drop some classes, and end up with a low grade in the three credits he didn't drop.

I am not sure college was a good fit for John.

The reason John liked his dorm room is that he had put in some custom hidden shelving. Nearly everyone in every dorm was 17, 18 or 19. John was 25. You had to be over 21 to buy beer. John was paying for his college by selling beer. As easy as falling off a log, except for the potential for fines and jail time.

John was also a prankster. One of John's pranks was to wrap himself up completely with toilet paper and have his roommate wheel him into the dining hall. The toilet paper looked like gauze, and nobody knew what was going on, so no one said anything as John's roommate fed John spoonful by spoonful through the tiny hole they had left for his mouth.

I was involved with one of John's pranks. Every Saturday night was steak night. Those who chose to have steak could cook it themselves on a large grill in the dining room. About 25 people could grill at the same time, as the grill was quite large. John found a dead mole. He gave it to me. When no one was looking, I put it out into the middle of the big grill. After about five minutes, one of the dining room workers got a very long set of tongs, and grabbed the mole off the grill. I loved his calm comment, "I think this one is done."

Years later, I ran into John. He eventually graduated, and became a junior high school teacher. He told me about the pranks he was pulling at his junior high, such as putting some other teacher's furniture on top of their carport. I am glad he found his proper place in the world.

Nearly Free Long Distance—For some reason everyone else in the dorm got a phone bill every month except my roommate and me. There was one phone in each room, and in theory you had to pay extra for long distance calls. At the time, long distance calls were expensive, at as much as 50 cents per minute to call the Seattle or Tacoma areas. Most students made long distance calls. Any student with family, boyfriends, girlfriends, etc. might pay a lot for long distance. At first we didn't notice, as we didn't know we were supposed to be getting a phone bill.

By June, we had a line out our door of people who wanted to use our phone. We made them all agree to pay us if we ever got a bill, but most said it was worth a try for possibly free long distance. We left in June having never gotten a bill.

In August after I had gone home for the summer, I got a letter that the envelope said was from the telephone company in their Tacoma audit office. My phone, of course, had been in Bellingham, over 100 miles from Tacoma. Inside that envelope was an entirely hand-written bill for April, but it had my old Bellingham phone number and a list of numbers my roommate and I had called and the time of each call, duration and cost. Good thing it was for April, because the lines didn't form at our door until May and June. I thought about fighting it, but decided to just pay it. It was for $88, which was a lot for a college student. I didn't even ask my roommate for his share. I never got another bill for my freshman year. Just the one hand-written bill from Tacoma for April. The only hand-written bill I have ever gotten from a phone company. I wish I had kept it. It might be worth $88 to a collector.

Saving Money on Rent in College—If you live with a bunch of other people you hardly know in a big house, as college students often do, see if you can get your messiest roommate to handle the rent, then everyone else pays him or her their share. About a week before the rent is due, razz this person about how messy their room is, just enough to get them a bit defensive. A week later, pay your share of rent by check. Always by check. Somewhere along the line, your roommate will lose one of your checks and be too embarrassed to ask you for another one.

Guess how I know....Hey Brian, I'll write you another check if you ask me to.

I didn't do it on purpose. I just noticed afterward how well it worked and why.

High School Soccer Coach—Due to my experience with the Chargers, and the fact that a neighbor of ours from Eastgate had taken the job of Principal at Sehome High School in Bellingham, I was asked to

be the first soccer coach at Sehome High School. It is tough to set up a new program. First of all, there were not quite enough boys for a full boys team (nine—you need eleven), but there were four girls who wanted to play, so we ended up with a coed team. There was no league. I contacted Bellingham High School (BHS), the only other high school in Bellingham at the time, and scheduled to play against them twice. I also had no car, but many of the players did, so I awkwardly asked the players for rides. It was also the case that most of the players were seniors, and I was just one year older than they were, including three of the four girls. I know as a coach I was not supposed to notice, but the girls were very good looking. (I have always been attracted to post-puberty females approximately my age, so I was not terribly attracted to the Chargers, who were mostly pre-puberty).

I could not find other high schools to play in the area other than BHS, so I set up some games with some community college teams. I was coaching a lot of beginners on my team, but at the community college level you don't typically find beginners. The games against BHS were competitive (but we lost—their program was all boys and not brand new). The games against the community college teams we got beaten pretty badly. Not something I wanted to put on my résumé: lost every game, lasted only one season. I did enjoy it, though.

Flying Referee— Dominic, the coach of the junior high school soccer program in Bellingham was almost always the referee at soccer games in the Bellingham area. I was one of only a few people who had taken referee training when I was at WWU and Dominic knew that. So one day I got a call from Dominic saying he couldn't referee a game at Lopez Island High School and wanted to know if I could do it. I told him sadly that I could not, because in order to make a 1 pm game, I would have to take the 10:15 ferry and I had a 10:30 mid-term test. How long is your test? He asked. An hour, I said. Could you be at the airport by noon? Yes, I said. Ok, do that, he said.

I had never been to the Bellingham Airport and didn't know what to expect. As I was driving there in a borrowed car, I was kicking myself for not getting better directions. No way would you just say I'll meet you at SeaTac airport, for example. SeaTac is too big.

I drove to the airport and I noticed three small planes lined up on the right side of the road. There was a man leaning against one of the small planes. I pulled up and got out of the car. "Are you Doug?" asked the man.

I had to sit in the copilot's seat, as that was the only other seat besides the pilot's in this small plane. It was a beautiful cloudless day, and flying over the San Juan Islands was spellbinding. "Do you want to fly for a while?" YES! (Duh). I took the controls for a few minutes, and tipped the wings a couple of times over the islands as the waters of Puget Sound sparkled below. Awesome.

The pilot landed without incident. Someone from the HS met me at the airport and drove me to the school. He looked at my crummy whistle and gave me a new one. Lopez Island HS lost 1-0 on a penalty kick I called. They were not happy but I think it was the correct call. It was the only time I was asked to referee a HS game in any of the San Juan Islands, and certainly the only time I was flown to a game.

A poor college student got a great plane flight, got to fly the plane, and they *paid me*.

Meeting Lorraine—I actually barely remember the first time Lorraine and I met. Someone introduced her to me as someone "from Idaho" and I thought she was cute, but a visitor I would probably never see again.

As noted earlier, I had not had much luck in the dating department. The nice thing about college dorms is that you can hang out in the dorms and meet a lot of people your age, though. I met dozens of very nice girls just walking around campus and in the dorms.

94

I was feeling sorry for myself one day in early June. I realized that my freshman year was coming to a close and I had not gone on a single date. I should go on at least one date, I told myself. I thought about all the girls I had met, and decided I would ask Jan—Lorraine's roommate—on a date. So I gathered my courage and went to Jan's room and knocked on the door. Lorraine answered and immediately said, "You probably want Jan. She has gone home for the year." Good thing she said this in this way. I thought to myself that my objective was to ask a girl on a date, and here was a cute girl I remembered from somewhere, so I said, "Actually, I was hoping to ask you to the movies."

Lorraine hesitated, and I could see it. I was getting ready to walk away, when she said "Sure."

Later, I found out from Lorraine that Jan thought I was the clod who wore floodies all the time and Jan didn't particularly like me, but another friend Cathy had said something nice about me. Lorraine was weighing Jan's and Cathy's comments. Thanks, Cathy.

My dating advice: Be considerate of the roommate. Or at least consider the roommate.

Hug Night—Lorraine and I went on a date, and it went well. We hit it off, and enjoyed the conversation afterward. Neither of us wanted the date to end. As a result, after returning Lorraine to her room, I stayed for a while. Remembering my first date with Cheryl and how I had inadvertently frightened her, I was extra careful with Lorraine.

Even though I didn't really want to go, I finally decided I really "should" go, so I gave Lorraine a hug goodbye. She didn't let go. I didn't either. We continued that hug until dawn.

We still call it "hug night."

2 am Scare—[Cousin Rick] I was a member of the cross-country team and the track team in high school, and I continued to run pretty much every night in college. I preferred to run in the evening, because that usually worked better for my schedule and I tended to overheat in the day. I did not like to skip a night, and tried to run at least a few miles every evening. One night we had been invited to a party, and I was unable to run before the party. The party let out about 1:30 am, and I decided to go for a five-mile run afterwards. This was not particularly unusual for me. What was unusual was that I found myself approaching a lone woman at 2 am under a dark noisy freeway underpass from behind. I didn't want to scare her, but I didn't see how I could avoid it. I chose to say in a loud voice "I am just jogging here!" as I approached her from behind. As I expected, she jumped and screamed as I went by, obviously scared half to death, then relieved as I kept going. I guess we could each ask the other what the heck we were doing there at 2 am.

One of only a few times I messed up on my promise to Cheryl not to frighten women.

Coaching Basketball—When I was at WWU I was hired as a coach for elementary school kids by the City of Bellingham. I got the job because of my coaching experience with the Chargers as well as coaching soccer at Sehome HS. I was asked to coach both girls and boys soccer teams. The girls' soccer team I coached did well, but the boys team did not, because I insisted that all players respect and help each other. (If there was a sportsmanship award, my teams usually got it). The teams were third-, fourth- and fifth-graders combined. A bunch of fourth- and fifth-grade boys refused to respect the third grade boys and quit. Fine with me. So my boys' team ended up being almost all third-graders playing against mostly older teams.

After the soccer season was done, I was still on the payroll, and they asked me to coach basketball. I am lousy at basketball. I kid you not, the name of my intramural basketball team in high school was "Rough's Bumblers" and my friend John got our team's highest point tally one game. He had all of our team's points, two, which he got on a jumper mid-way through the second half.

In my defense, I discovered later that my problem was that I practiced shooting baskets without glasses then played basketball games with them on. I had astigmatism, which means my uncorrected eyes saw things like hoops slightly over from where they really were. When I practiced, I accounted for that. In a game, all of my shots were off because I wore glasses. That is what I tell myself in any case.

Anyhow, I was an awful basketball player and had never coached basketball.

I was a trooper, though, and I got the kids together and made up drills as I went along. Fortunately, I had very few beginners, and most had played on other teams for years.

During the second practice for the girls team, Amy, a fifth-grade girl took me aside and very nicely said, "Look, coach, we kinda already know how to play. We have played for a few years now. Can you just let us play?"

From that point on, I took all my coaching cues from Amy.

My, or I should say Amy's girls' basketball team won the Bellingham city championship.

Mr. Steak—One of several college jobs I had was as a waiter at Mr. Steak. I learned some of my most important life's lessons as a waiter:

First, if you are having a bad day, you had better pretend you are having a good day, or you will not get good tips. Nobody wants to hear you complain.

Second, do your rushing out of sight of the customer. Near the customer appear precise and appreciative.

Third, do what is needed to make the customer happy. We had two people with bugs in their salad in one night. One got a fresh salad and was happy. The other got the bill for her entire party taken care of in order for her to be happy. I asked the manager why the first woman did not get her bill taken care of and he said, "Because she is happy."

The only free food we got at Mr. Steak was either one baked potato or one salad per shift. If we wanted a steak, a full meal or a dessert, we had to pay for it.

Jana was a waitress who was nasty to the folks she worked with, but nauseatingly drippy sweet to the customers. Jana got the best tips.

Irene was the smartest. She got good tips without being mean to the folks she worked with. She was the only other person at the restaurant in college. One day I saw Irene cutting cakes. We had very fancy cakes delivered for dessert and we cut them up into 16 pieces. I saw Irene take a knife and start cutting one of the cakes from the middle outward. At first I thought "that is dumb, why doesn't she cut all the way through, that way she will only need 8 cuts?" But then I realized that Irene was the smart one, so I kept watching. She carefully cut each piece the same size, but when she was done, there were 17 pieces. She ate the 17th piece. I knew she was smart!

Don was the dishwasher. Don had been washing dishes for 20 years! He was always singing in the noisy dish room, but usually songs he made up. One time I brought dirty dishes back to Don and he was singing, "My wife is a hippo…"

Spaceman was our most consistent customer. I don't know his real name. He came every day for the 99 cent special. If anyone listened, he talked about government mind control through our coffee cups, pie wedge murders, how he was Jesus Christ 29 lifetimes ago and the need to keep windows open 17.5 inches at night for certain auras to fit just right. I was the only male waiter, and they always sat Spaceman in my section, because he made the women nervous and he would hold your table for two hours for a 15-cent tip. I was told he suffered trauma from the Vietnam war.

Mr. Steak did not serve liquor. Directly across the street was the Black Angus restaurant, which was a steakhouse that served liquor. I knew waitresses there that made twice what we made in tips.

One Saturday night at about 7 pm an obviously drunk couple was seated in my section. They both picked up their menus and pretended to read them. I say pretended, because both menus were upside down. When I greeted them, the man said he would like two martinis. I apologized that we did not serve liquor. He leaned forward and said as clearly as his slurred speech would allow, "Two mar-TEE-nees!" Again, I apologized that we did not serve liquor. He reacted as though I had slapped him in the face. "I am so sorry my dear!" he said to the woman he was with and they both closed their upside down menus and stumbled out the door.

A locally legendary story from one of the waitresses at the Black Angus across the street: It seems a certain waitress who had been at Black Angus for many years had a large table of Canadians seated in her section for lunch. They ran her ragged with order changes, extra ketchup, etc. She says she gave them great service anyway, but they left her no tip. At dinner the same day, the same group asked to be sat in her section. She refused. The group insisted. She still refused. The group had the manager tell her she had to serve them. She quit. The manager ended up serving the group. Nobody knew if the manager got tipped, but most folks suspect not. This was a legendary story because the waiters in Bellingham, near the border with Canada, had a local joke: What is the difference between a canoe and a Canuck? Canoes tip.

Computer Center—Another job I had at WWU was working at the computer center. This was when computers were twice the size of a large

freezer and you used decks of oversized cards with holes punched in them to get them to work. Things seem slightly different now.

Years later I was walking downtown at lunch as I always did and someone came up to me, called me by name and said he had worked at the computer center with me. I did not remember him, but I was too embarrassed to say that. He grabbed me and took me to his office, and introduced me to everyone in his office, including his boss. I just kept saying "Hi, I am Doug"—I never learned his name and I was too embarrassed to ask.

Attempted Robbery—In May of my senior year in college, Lorraine and I were staying overnight at Lorraine's grandmother's house in South Seattle on a weekend. At about 9 pm on a Saturday night, we decided to go to Lorraine's mother's house about six blocks away. Lorraine wanted to drive because she said it was a "bad area" but I said it was a nice night at about 70 degrees and we should walk. We walked.

It was a lovely walk, and as we went around the next-door neighbor's rock wall to go up Lorraine's mother's driveway, I was about to say, "See, it is not such a bad area" when we looked up to the deck over the driveway and saw Lorraine's mother screaming and hitting a man dressed in dark clothes. The front door opened to the deck over the driveway and both were fighting in front of the front door.

Lorraine ran around to the side door to call 911. Smart. I ran up onto the deck. Not so smart.

The guy started to run toward me and I tackled him to the deck. He hit me in the head with something metal and I was shaken for a moment. When I cleared my head, the would-be robber was on his hands and knees on the deck and Lorraine's mother was still screaming and hitting him, doing what looked like absolutely no damage whatsoever. Lorraine's grandfather was now on the deck holding onto the guy's butt trying to keep him on his knees.

I have played soccer pretty much all my life. I kicked him in the head. I had flimsy shoes, and my shoe failed. My foot came completely through the front of my shoe. I am pretty sure I hurt this guy's head as much as he had hurt my head.

At this point, he fired his shotgun.

The sudden blast didn't seem to hit anyone but surprised us, and the guy jumped to his feet and ran toward the end of the deck where there was no stairs or way out. The only thing he could do from there was turn and fire again. I realized that and felt like my only option was to chase him. I grabbed his shotgun barrel and pointed it to the sky, then grabbed the other end of the shotgun. We were both facing the same direction, and I was now holding the shotgun across his chest. I still had not seen his face. I could see through the door that Lorraine was on the phone with the police.

I suddenly realized that this guy was not trying to push on the shotgun and was trying to get his right hand around behind him toward me. This set off alarms in my head. I thought he had a knife and was going to stab me.

I was wrong. He had a pistol and was trying to shoot me.

I was bigger than this guy, and I was stronger, too, probably due to adrenaline. I picked him up and threw him over the deck railing head-first toward the driveway below.

In my mind I still see him in slow motion dropping his two guns and catching the bottom railing of the deck so that he swung around and landed on his feet. Damn! At this point I saw the shotgun and pistol, along with burglary tools and some jewelry that all landed next to him. I started to go over the railing and was going to jump on him because if he went for the guns we were sitting ducks up on the deck. Instead of going for the guns, he ran.

I didn't jump off the deck. I realized that he had hit me in the head with either a shotgun or a pistol.

The police showed up about one minute later. Sixty seconds seemed like an hour at the time. The guy had run toward a park with lots of trails only a few blocks away, and by the time the police got dogs to track him in the park, he had escaped.

The police interviewed all of us: Lorraine, Lorraine's mom, her grandfather and me. It took a couple of hours. After about 45 minutes, someone sheepishly climbed out of the bushes in the yard.

What happened before we got there: The robber went to the front door on the deck over the driveway. Lorraine's mom undid about five locks to open the door. He pointed a pistol at her and said "Get in the house." She instead started screaming and lunged at him. He fired the pistol, which did not hit her but narrowly missed someone in the street, who climbed into the bushes to escape the madness. We came around the corner at this point. We had not heard the pistol shot because we were behind the rock wall.

The police later arrested a suspect, but none of us could pick him out of a lineup. I never saw the guy's face myself. He was Hispanic and about five inches shorter than me, or about 5' 8". And he didn't wash his hair very often. That is all I know for sure.

The guy in the bushes did not look. I think he was too busy crapping his pants.

The police did not let us keep any of the stuff the guy dropped, for some reason.

For many years it was "Hey, kids! Let's visit grandma's house and find the shotgun blast hole in the deck."

Neighbor Girl at College—In June of my senior year in college, just before I graduated, I saw the girl who lived next door to me in Eastgate hanging off her boyfriend in the main plaza carrying textbooks. She is five or six years younger than me, but apparently part of some "head start" program. When I left for college she had been in elementary school. My first thought was "I gotta get outta here."

GETTING MARRIED

Honeymoon Before Wedding—We planned our honeymoon before our wedding. Lorraine and I had so much in common that we starting making long-term plans together. We both wanted to take a trip across the country in the summer while we were in college. We wanted to camp and stay with relatives to make the trip affordable. After thinking about staying with relatives, we thought we would be much more welcome if we were on our honeymoon than if we were just engaged. So, we needed to get married before our trip, so the trip would not just be couch-surfing, it could be a honeymoon. That is how it came together.

My parents had been founding members of a church just a few blocks from where I grew up. That seemed like the obvious place to get married, except we both wanted to get married outside. We could not count on good weather, so we planned an outside wedding in the garden behind the church, so that if it rained we could easily go inside. It threatened, but it did not rain. We had planned to have an audio recording of the wedding, but forgot the tape recorder. Lorraine said she wanted it taped, and would not go down the "aisle" (a trail, because we were outside) until a tape recorder was found. My brother Jim ran home and got a tape recorder. A friend of ours, Susan, sang songs she had not rehearsed and played her guitar while my brother went to get his tape recorder. We were winging it. When Jim got back, we started.

Lorraine's brother Gary wrote a song for the occasion, "Song for Sister" and sang it.

The minister read the vows from a different wedding, not the ones we had chosen for our wedding. But he got our names correct, so it was fine.

Our wedding night we spent in my brother's basement playing poker with some friends. We used curlers in place of chips.

Lorraine was 19. I was 20. It was our very first wedding.

Forty years later, we went back to find the garden behind the church where our wedding took place. Rather than a lovely garden, we found a shed and some old tires.

Weddings and Toilet Paper—At the time we got married, it

was standard for people to generally mess up the bride and groom's car with toilet paper, shaving cream, etc. Not sure how that got started.

My uncle Stu told the story of how he wanted to avoid that problem, because he was going to use his car to travel between California where he lived and Ohio where Harriet's parents lived. Stu rented a garage clear across town a full month before his wedding. He took the bus to work for a month while his car sat in a garage across town. After Stu and Harriet got married, they took a taxi to the garage, where he found his car covered in shaving cream and toilet paper up on blocks with the tires missing. (Over 70 years later, I found out that Stu's cousin Stuart Wilson was the culprit).

Another friend told us of getting married and having someone put smelly cheese in their car's vents. Someone else said their friends accidently broke a window in their "decorating" enthusiasm. Others told similar horror stories.

For my wedding, I was paranoid. My friends included Alex (See *Alex's Pipe Bomb*) and Mark (See *Mark's Firework*). We were going to drive to Maine and back in our car. So, I told no one, not even Lorraine where the car was. I parked the car in a neighborhood a mile from the church and walked to the church along a route I knew no one else would take on my wedding day. Unfortunately I accidently left the tape recorder in the car, but I didn't go back and get it or tell anyone where it was.

We got a ride to our reception at Lake Sammamish State Park and rented a canoe. We told our friends they could put toilet paper and shaving cream on our canoe rather than our car. So they did. At the park we ordered 7 extra large pizzas and 100 pieces of KFC chicken delivered to our reception. The pizzas were gone in less than five minutes (our friends were college kids) and we ate a lot of chicken on our honeymoon.

Three Marriages—One thing Lorraine and I have in common is that we have each been married three times.

To each other.

The first time, we invited relatives and friends, including the entire Chargers girls soccer team that I had coached. It was a good-sized wedding.

The second time, on our tenth anniversary, we only invited the people we had invited to our original wedding who were unable to attend. It was a very small wedding.

On the 100th birthday of Kirkland, the city had a special: a full wedding ceremony in the park, flowers, cake, photographer and a tour-boat catered reception for only $100 plus $100 per invited guest.

We didn't invite anyone to our third wedding, not even our kids—we only paid $100. It was a VERY small wedding.

HONEYMOON

No Reservation Camping at Yellowstone—We took a
honeymoon trip driving across the country on our honeymoon. We
arrived at a full popular campground Yellowstone National Park late in the
evening in late June and did not have a reservation. No problem. I found
someone with a small tent who had a standard (big) campsite. I told them
I would pay for their site if we could use just a small section of it in the
corner. And by the way, we were on our honeymoon.

It worked.

Honeymoon Cash—In 1977, our honeymoon summer, credit cards
were only for expensive hotels, posh restaurants and other high-priced
things. No grocery stores took credit cards, nor did the cheaper gas
stations, nor did campgrounds. And "out-of-town" checks were nearly
universally refused. As a result, even though we were broke college
students, our honeymoon was pretty much entirely paid with cash.

Hence camping and couch-surfing with relatives. In forty nights, we
stayed only one night in a hotel, and it was $12 for the night. It was in
Paul, Idaho, which I found out later was where my dad was born.

Outrageous Gas Price—We tried very hard to get the very best
gas prices, as gas was a big part of our expenses on our honeymoon trip
across the US in 1977. However, Yellowstone horrified us. We could not
avoid buying gas in Yellowstone at the outrageous price of 72.9 cents per
gallon!

Camping in Mitchell, South Dakota—We stopped at

Mitchell, South Dakota and found a spot not too far from the highway to camp. It wasn't an official camping spot, we were just tired of driving and it was about time to sleep. While setting up the tent, the mosquitoes were a problem. They got worse. Finally, we found that there were too many that had made it inside our mosquito netting so that we just could not sleep. Plus, Lorraine had gotten bitten badly around her eyes.

We decided to leave, but taking down the tent meant getting even more bitten. With a small car, normally getting the camping equipment compacted tightly is important, but we grabbed the tent, stakes, poles, tarps and sleeping bags in a big wadded mess and stuffed it in the car in a big hurry, swearing and swiping all the way.

We drove through the night to our next stop, where we had planned to stay with my dad's great aunt and cousin in Wilmette, Illinois, just north of Chicago.

We arrived at about 7 am. I knocked on the door. At that point, Lorraine's face had swollen up around her eyes so much from mosquito bites that she could not see.

This is my lovely bride. Her face is not usually red, bumpy and swollen and normally she can see, honest.

Lunch with a Caterer—My dad's cousin Cassie was a caterer in

Wilmette, IL in the Chicago area. She also had five sons at home, all either teenagers or in their early 20s. She set out lunch for us the first day we were there on our honeymoon. Beautiful buffet setting on a large, interesting table. I didn't want to touch it because it looked so amazing. I went to get my camera. By the time I got my camera, the boys had gotten their lunch.

Well, I'll just have to remember how amazing it was. I was lucky there was any food left.

Niagara Falls on July 1—Friday, July 1, 1977 was Canada Day, and Monday, July 4 of course was a holiday in the US—when there is a weekend between the two holidays Niagara Falls on the border is popular on July 1. Who knew?

A little over a mile from the falls parking lot, after moving about two car lengths in 20 minutes, we just pulled over and parked by the side of the highway and walked.

Nice falls. A bit crowded.

Maine Idea—When you start your honeymoon trip in Washington state and tell people you plan to drive across the US, for some reason we had to go to Maine. We did, and just a few yards past the "Welcome to Maine" sign we took a photo and headed back to stay with some relatives in Connecticut.

Somehow, telling Seattle folks you drove from Seattle to Connecticut is just not as impressive as telling them you drove to Maine.

Best Stories—I asked every older relative we saw on our honeymoon for their best story and we brought a tape recorder to record it. It was one of those ideas that sounds great in theory, but ends up being disappointing in practice. I will not bore you with most of these "best stories." (You spilled a pail of milk? You are 85 years old and that's the best you got?). I was glad I taped my grandfather, though.

Grandpa in World War I—My mother's father William Houghton was quite the character. Perfect eyesight his entire life, well into his mid-80s, he read the newspaper every day without glasses. We interviewed him on our honeymoon and we asked him for his best story.

Born in 1896, Yale class of 1916, he enlisted in the Army as a private and was an engineer—one of those folks who supported the troops mostly by rebuilding destroyed bridges and roads. He was in B Company and told me that everyone was awakened every morning by someone blowing a bugle. This was standard in the Army during WWI. It was a pretty simple song. It was called "First Call" or "Reveille" and it meant you had to report for duty. My grandfather told me that most people think they know the song, but you might be surprised that it is often not the tune you thought it was. (Find "First Call" or "Reveille" on the internet and see if it is the tune you thought it was.) Anyway, the guy who played the song in his company jazzed it up so much they wrote a song about him. Can you guess the name? Yes, it is the "Boogie Woogie Bugle Boy of Company B."

One day toward what turned out to be a few months before the end of the war, fighting intensified and my grandfather's unit found themselves close to the front lines. They were hunkered down in France not far from the current French-German border, while the Germans were about a mile away. There was a report that his sergeant was wounded, lying in "No Man's Land" between the lines. His wounds were not fatal, but he could not walk. He and a fellow soldier decided to put on "red cross" arm bands, grab a stretcher and attempt to rescue the sergeant. After putting the wounded sergeant on the stretcher, they were captured by the Germans. By this time in the war, the Germans were running out of men of military age. As a result, they were escorted to the Prisoner of War Camp by a lone boy who looked to be all of 13 years old.

It was about a four-mile hike to the POW camp, and the entire way my grandfather looked at the back of this 13-year-old's neck, while thinking of the hidden 12-inch knife strapped to the back of his calf. The kid had not searched him well. He chose not to kill the boy.

A few months later the war was over and he was sent home mostly unharmed. But more than 60 years later, he could still remember the back of that boy's neck and the four-mile mental struggle he had.

I never would have heard this story had I not asked. A true hero, Gramp did not toot his own horn. Or bugle.

The Family Difference—On our honeymoon trip across the country we were welcomed with open arms by family members from both sides of the family, even when they had never seen us before. We were family, and they loved us. We had planned the trip around staying with relatives with the hope that this would be the case, and it was. One double-fourth cousin (I think) took us on a boat ride. However, in the Washington, DC area, we could not find relatives to stay with and camping was not an option, so we stayed with the parents of a college friend.

What a difference! "The towels are over there. Try not to be noisy as we have to get up early tomorrow" was pretty much the entire conversation we had with them. We left as soon as we could.

Lesson learned: If you spent the night at some random person's house claim you are a distant cousin. They'll probably treat you well. Who knows what your great-grandparents might have done? Maybe you are.

A Nice Dress—We stayed in a former plantation in Ware Neck, Virginia. The driveway was about a quarter-mile long. There were three buildings, the old slave quarters, which had been turned into equipment storage for horses, the old servant's quarters, which was now the new servant's quarters (a pretty nice two-story house), and the mansion itself, which of course was huge with a nice view of Chesapeake Bay. Lorraine's great uncle (her father's father's brother) hosted us along with three of his grandkids. There was plenty of room, and maids to boot.

The thing I remember most about our stay was being instructed to sit in the living room for a few minutes before dinner. Lorraine and I, the three grandkids and Lorraine's great uncle all were to sit and wait in the living room facing the stairway. After about 15 minutes, Lorraine's great aunt came sweeping down the stairway wearing a nice dress. No one told us specifically, but I think appreciating that dress was why we were supposed to wait.

When someone hosts you on your honeymoon in a mansion, the least you can do is tell them they have a nice dress.

Honeymooning in Nebraska—It was the hottest summer in decades. We left the east coast and we did not have air conditioning in our little car so we thought it might be cooler if we drove at night. I remember one obnoxiously enthusiastic radio station personality saying that it was exactly midnight, and the temperature was 98 and the humidity was 96. I wanted to throw something at the radio.

Our next scheduled stop was my father's cousin's farm in Nebraska, the one that Walker Bates had homesteaded. We were about two hours away and called about 10 am to tell them we planned to check into a hotel to sleep as we had driven through the night. Betty and Ivan would not have us stay in a hotel, and insisted we come straight to the farm if we thought we could go another two hours, and there we could eat, freshen up and sleep. We did.

We arrived just before noon. We went into the dining room where there was a huge table that looked as though it would easily seat 16 people. It was full of dishes of food. Chicken, beef, pork, vegetables, fruit, ice cream, desserts, you name it. I remember Betty saying with a straight face, "I am sorry but the potatoes are store bought. Our potatoes didn't come up this year." It turned out that everything else had been grown on the farm. The chicken, for example, had been alive less than an hour earlier.

We gently told them that they had gone a bit overboard with too much food, but they told us they don't get many honeymooners in Nebraska.

Second Honeymoon—On our 40th Anniversary, Lorraine and I went on a second honeymoon. On our first honeymoon we drove all the way across the country and on our second we drove half way across the country. We followed most of the same roads from Seattle to the mid-west and back that we did on our original honeymoon. The main difference was on the first honeymoon we camped and couch-surfed, while on the second honeymoon we did airbnb and we insisted on air conditioning and wifi.

Another difference was that on the original honeymoon we saw 14 cops doing speed traps the entire trip. Of those 14 speed traps, 11 were in Washington State. Compare that to forty years later in 2017 when we saw 19 cops doing speed traps, of which 13 were in Washington State. Washington still "wins" the speed trap race. What is amazing is that Washington has the worst traffic, so most of the time you cannot even go the speed limit, much less exceed it.

What is the secret of staying married for forty years? Complete forgiveness. Lorraine is very good at this. Good thing, too.

We saw homesteaded farm-owner Betty (Ivan is long gone) who looks about the same 40 years later. I hope I look as good as she does after 40 more years.

All the other relatives we stayed with 40 years previously are, shall we say, no longer hosting visitors.

On our original honeymoon Lorraine and I had fond memories of sharing a peanut buster parfait at a Dairy Queen in Cody, Wyoming. So we found that Dairy Queen and told them we had returned on our second honeymoon after 40 years, and were again going to share a peanut buster parfait. Ok, said the 16-year-old behind the counter. Here. Next!

I am not sure what I expected, but it wasn't that.

SEATTLE CITY LIGHT

From College to a Job—I went out of my way in college—I don't think this is unusual—to avoid having early morning classes. I was not a morning guy.

I had a tough time finding a job after college. Had I known I was going to get three job offers in September, I might have enjoyed the summer after I graduated, but I spent that summer sending out resumes and trying to get interviews. One of the first places I applied was Boeing, through the normal process. In September, I mentioned to my dad that I had applied at Boeing through the normal process and he asked for my resume. The next day he had an offer from Boeing. As it turned out, I also got two other offers at about the same time. Three offers in three days. Merrill Lynch, Boeing and Seattle City Light (SCL). I took the SCL offer because it offered the highest initial pay. Boeing's offer from my dad was not bad, and I probably would have taken that had I not had the SCL offer.

When I got the call from SCL, they told me to report to work at eight the next day. I admit I asked "in the morning?"

After I had been at SCL for about a year, I got an offer from Boeing through the normal process. It was for $5.40 per hour (not much above minimum wage at the time and less than a third of my SCL pay), in Kansas. They would not help me move to Kansas. Hmmm. Move to Kansas to get less than one-third of my current pay with no moving expense help. Tough decision.

Failed Assignment—My first assignment at SCL was to write a computer model of the Seattle hydroelectric system. I actually think my boss couldn't think of something for me to do, so he gave me that assignment as a time-filler.

I couldn't do it. It was far too complex for me to write a model by myself in one month. But I think it was the most important failure I ever had at SCL.

One month after my first assignment, my boss came to me completely unconcerned that I had not finished my task and never again asked me about it. He had a set of other tasks for me. He and I were to write a Strategic Resource Plan, and I had a number of things to do to help get this document published. My time spent trying to figure out how to correctly model the system was a great help to me in putting together the Strategic Resource Plan and in many ways it helped me for all of my future tasks.

In my work later on SCL's Financial Planning Model, Strategic Planning Model, Capital Improvements Model and many others, the insights I got from that "failed" assignment came in handy.

I am told that failing on a first assignment is not always a good thing. I wouldn't know.

Lee Speaking—When I first started SCL, everyone had a phone on their desk, but there were only two incoming lines. One of those lines was only for the director. If someone outside of SCL wanted to call any of the other twelve folks in our office, they called the second line, and Lee answered.

I sat near Lee, and I heard her answer the phone all day long. She always slowly said exactly the same thing: "Power Management, Lee speaking." Then, no matter what the caller said, she would reply: "Oh, let me see, please hold the line."

All day, many times a day. And did I mention slowly?

The Good News Story—When I had been at SCL for a few months, I ran into a guy who had a Good News Story that he just had to tell everyone. He had made a Smart Decision and wanted everyone he met it seemed, including me, to hear about it. Ten years earlier, during the worst of the Boeing Bust in the Seattle area, he had run across a big house in West Seattle with a nice view. That house was selling for $4000. That was just not right. That was too low. So he bought it. Now, ten years later in 1980, the Good News Story was that he had just sold that house for $14,000 making a $10,000 profit. It was the Smart Decision, and he wanted everyone to know.

Not that it matters, but in 2017 the house sold for $2.8 million.

"Hungry" People—If you go for a walk in downtown Seattle every lunch like I did for 30 years, you will inevitably run into people begging for money. They nearly always say that they are "hungry." My lunchtime walk often involved walking to the Pike Place Market and buying some fruit to eat while walking. I would give these "hungry" people some fruit and every time except once, they were confused or angry—often tossing it on the ground—reminding me that they had asked for money, not food. When I reminded them that they had said they were hungry, they looked sheepish, angry or disgusted. Once, only once, a woman took my banana and said "finally, g—damn something to eat" and walked off. Unspoken were "thank" and "you."

One guy had his hand out and begged me for money so often, I told him "I recognize you. You can recognize me. I'll never give you money, so save your breath." After that, he would respectfully nod at me as I walked by, and I would respectfully nod back.

My favorite two times were: Once when I pointed out to someone with a sign that said simply "I am hungry" that free breakfast cereal was being passed out across the street, he told me "I don't like that kind of cereal."

The other time was when a man and woman approached me and told me their car broke down on a freeway exit ramp and they needed money to get it towed. I knew that the ramp where they said their car was had a blind curve, so I knew the police would want to put some kind of flashing lights there so exiting cars would know it was there. I told them that they were in luck that the police station was just one block away and the police would be glad to help them protect their car. The man immediately said angrily, "I can't believe you don't believe my story!" I said, "Well, I guess I don't believe it now!"

Homeless Cheryl—One day at lunch I passed a woman on the street with her hand out that looked like it might be the adult version of a girl I had in my kindergarten class. "Cheryl?" I asked as I walked by. She didn't say anything, and I kept walking. About a block later, she caught up with me. "I thought you were a cop." She said. It was indeed Cheryl from my kindergarten class, now a homeless adult. I offered to buy her a coffee at a nearby Starbucks to talk. When we got there, she said she didn't need coffee, so we just sat and I heard her story.

She talked fast and mentioned a lot of names I did not know. She alternated between being angry and matter-of-fact. She and her mom had become homeless around first or second grade and she had been forced to change schools. She had a long list of people to blame for where she was. Nothing was her fault. Being homeless was difficult, but she got used to it and even preferred it in some ways. She seemed to distain people with "garbage disposals and garage door openers" (ahem, like me). She seemed to think she was somehow entitled to the money that the government was giving her each month for some kind of disability I could not detect, and was pretty upset that each month this money was at risk to be taken away from her. She had had at least one terminated pregnancy, possibly more. It did not sound like she had a great life to me, but she also seemed to have no desire to attain a "garage door opener" life either. I got the impression that drugs were involved, but I didn't ask.

After talking for about twenty minutes, she mentioned that I had offered to buy her a cup of coffee that would have cost about $3. Could she instead have that $3 in cash? This was the only time I gave $3 to a homeless person in my 30 years of lunchtime walks. I paid Cheryl for her story.

I bet she did not buy coffee with that $3. Tea, maybe?

David's Keys—[TF] I worked with a guy named David back in the days when computers were expensive enough that not everyone had one. We had a "pod" of eight computers to handle the needs of about twelve of us. It worked out okay. Those who needed the computers for nearly all of their work, like David, went to the pod area as soon as they got to their desk. In David's case, he put his key chain on his desk and went to the pod.

Phil was a prankster, and Phil's father's business had burned down a few months earlier. Phil grabbed all the keys from his dad's old business. Phil noted that David had 11 keys on his keychain, and was pretty certain that David would not notice if Phil added a key. Sure enough, David did not notice. So, Phil added another, then another.

A few weeks later, I went to lunch with David, Michelle and a couple of other folks from my group. Michelle pulled out a large key chain with about eight keys and I saw that David was watching her and listening to our conversation. I challenged Michelle to name what each key did. Michelle was able to do so. David got a far-off look in his eyes and noted that he was looking at his key chain the other day, and "I don't know what half those keys do." He was exactly right, because at that point Phil had told me David had 22 keys on his key chain, of which 11 were from Phil's dad's burned-out business.

Phil wished he had been able to hear this conversation in person.

About a week later, David's key chain was back to 11 keys. He told someone else in the office that he decided to remove the keys he "hardly ever used."

Pranking Phil—I was a computer programmer back when few people could do much with computers. In our office long ago, we did not have enough computers for everyone, so folks had to share. Phil found that the "big boss" had a computer just outside his office, but he never used it, and I doubt he knew how. Phil was one of the few people brave enough to use it, so it seemed like Phil almost had exclusive use of it.

Phil was the office prankster, so I decided to prank him one day. I set up the computer so that no matter what he did, the computer came back with "Phil is a jerk." I watched from afar as he clearly seemed to try everything including turning it off and back on, but the computer kept coming back with "Phil is a jerk." Suddenly, the "big boss" came off the elevator heading toward his office approaching Phil and the computer on his left and his office door on his right. Phil suddenly put all his papers over the computer screen. The big boss was preoccupied and did not notice, but I did.

Hiring Pete—When we went to hire a certain position at City Light, we interviewed a guy named Pete who seemed perfect for the job. The only problem with Pete was that he lived in a small town a little over two hours drive away from Seattle. We worried about his ability to show up early in the morning with a long commute. We decided that we would have a second interview with Pete at 7 am the following day. If Pete was on time, he would be hired.

Pete didn't know it, but he got the job at 6:57 am, three minutes before the interview started.

Lumberjack Programmer—[Cousin Rick] From Pete's resume, I saw he had spent many years as a lumberjack before beginning to program computers. I asked Pete why he switched from being a lumberjack to programming. He said because a huge falling log one day rolled onto him. He was hospitalized, more or less immobilized for several months. He had nothing to do during that time but read. He chose to read about computer programming.

So, he started his programming career with a "log on." Yes, that is an awful joke. Mine, not his. Pete is too nice a guy to say something like that.

Forks Real Estate—Pete told me about the house he bought in Forks, WA. This was a town that later became famous due to the Twilight book and movie series, but at the time was a fairly unknown town. He had purchased a house for $7000 and held it for seven years. When he went to sell, he fixed it up. After eight months trying to get a fair price, he finally sold for $5500.

Moral of the story: It is possible to buy a house for $7000, hold it for seven years, fix it up, then LOSE money when you sell it.

An and Anh—[Cousin Rick] City Light hired several "student engineers" each year. These were local college students usually in some engineering program who were hired temporarily, usually full time during the summer and part time during the school year.

At one point we had two student engineers from Vietnam, one named An and the other Anh. To most Americans, both of these names sounded like the word "on" but the two men claimed they are actually two different names.

One person in the office suggested that we call them "Up on" and "Down on" or "Left on" and "Right on" or pick one to be "off" to tell them apart. I think they meant those comments to be humorous. One day I decided to try and pronounce all three letters of Anh's name, breathing an "h" sound without a vowel as best I could at the end. "That's it!" He cried. "I have never heard an American who could pronounce my name before!"

Nick from North Vietnam—I worked with folks from other utilities in my job and so got a chance to hear their stories. One such person was a guy born in North Vietnam, now an American citizen who called himself Nick because it was easier than having folks try and pronounce his given name. Nick told me that American bombing raids happened in his town a lot as a kid. As a result, his town never used lights at night, for fear that they would guide bombing raids. The most light he ever saw at night was a candle, and even that was rare. The tallest building he ever saw in North Vietnam was two stories.

One night when he was about ten years old, his father decided to pay someone to get them out of North Vietnam, as refugees. Nick's family, along with several other families, were left on a raft in the Hong Kong shipping lanes, where the police would find them. Sure enough, at about 11 pm one night the police towed their raft to Macau.

Macau, as you may recall, is the largest gambling center in the world— much larger than Las Vegas. The multi-colored lights in Macau are similar to Vegas, except they go up the sides of 30 to 50 story buildings. For a ten-year-old boy who had never seen a three-story building and had rarely seen the light of a candle, arriving in Macau at night was, to put it mildly, stunning.

Two Quarters—We hired a new employee who put two quarters in the middle of his desk on his first day. I asked him why. He said he wanted to see if he needed to lock up. A few days later, those quarters were gone.

He locked his stuff in his desk every day and night.

Kathy the Intern—I sat next to a student intern named Kathy a few years after I started at SCL. At the time, SCL hired many student interns, kept them for 18 months then said goodbye and hired another. Kathy was one of several interns I had worked with at SCL. Unlike other interns, however, Kathy was doing far more work and as the end of her 18 months approached, it became clear that her leaving was going to be tougher than other interns leaving.

I went to my boss and mentioned that we should figure out a way to hire her permanently. This was not standard. It was not easy to do, but he did it. She is still working for the City of Seattle at this writing.

Later, we got another intern named Cindy who was quite sharp as well. When the end of Cindy's internship came up, I went to my boss again and he interrupted me to say that he was ahead of me on Cindy. She, too, still works for the City of Seattle.

Years later, Kathy was involved in the making of a documentary featured in the 2019 Seattle International Film Festival called "Engineering With Nature" about the effort to restore Thornton Creek in Seattle. At one point, 95% of the salmon entering Thornton Creek died, and Kathy spearheaded the effort to improve the creek to help salmon survive. When I went with Kathy to look at some of the work that was being done, I realized that we were going down a long one-lane road toward Larry's house. Larry was a guy I had played poker with decades earlier and I had been to his house just once, but I remembered a creek passing almost under his deck in the back.

Larry's house was gone. The city had bought it and torn it out, part of the creek restoration. Who knew that Larry's house and deck were part of the problem?

Inside Dams—Not many people get to go inside large dams.
Working for a hydroelectric company, I did. Most large dams have some kind of walkway inside them. Two large dams and one small dam stick out in my mind. When I went inside the Cedar Falls dam, just west of Seattle, I was a bit worried. Although it is concrete and has been inspected many times for integrity, it is very wet inside. Dripping everywhere and slippery. Made me nervous.

By contrast, the Ross dam in the North Cascades National Park area is dry and dusty inside. It is somehow reassuring to see dust inside a 400-foot high dam.

Rocky Brook is a very small dam on the Olympic Peninsula of Washington. So small that if it suddenly failed, it is unlikely anyone would be harmed. Unlike most dams which are built by utilities, this one was built by a developer incented by a government tax incentive. Inside the dam's powerhouse water was spraying everywhere!

Chinese Restaurant in Canada—Seattle City Light's Boundary
dam is one mile from Canada, and 12 miles from Idaho in the northeastern corner of Washington State, nowhere near population centers. The biggest nearby town is Metaline, population about 35. Restaurant choices are few. I was with a group from Seattle assigned to do work at the Boundary dam for a few days, and someone mentioned on the second day that there was a Chinese restaurant in Canada not too far away. Not knowing anything about it, we thought we might try it. As it happened, the border guard at the US/Canada border crossing looked to be of Chinese decent. After she asked the four of us all the usual

questions, we told her we were headed toward this Chinese restaurant that we didn't know anything about. What did she think of it? She said, "You guys said you are all from Seattle, right?" We said yes. She said, "Go back to Seattle."

WTO Riots—Downtown Seattle is a fun and festive place to walk around in mid-December, except when there are riots. Not that there were many riots, but the WTO riots of 1999 made my lunchtime walk less fun and festive. The mayor's attempts to control things failed pretty badly, such as the Mayor's Proclamation #3 that the National Guard surround a 23-block area around the WTO convention including the city's largest shopping area and not allow anyone in unless they were an employee, a delegate, or police. I was not allowed to go in because I was a mere customer trying to eat lunch. Directly behind the guardsman who would not let me pass were the "Dickens Carolers" joyfully singing in their merry costumes. They got in because they were employees. Not sure who they were singing to—maybe the National Guard.

Sept. 11, 2001—We don't normally watch TV in the morning, but we heard on the radio about the news out of New York. We turned on the TV just in time to see the second plane hitting the World Trade Center. I decided to go to work anyway, but Lorraine was worried about me working in the second tallest building in Seattle, across the street from the tallest building. She was worried enough that she came downtown early to meet me for a long lunch. She picked me up very early to take me to a restaurant away from downtown Seattle for a long lunch. I thought she was overreacting, but I went.

Later, we found out that there had in fact been a plan to have planes hit the two tallest buildings in Seattle on 9/11, but the terrorists did not have enough people to carry out that plan. Lorraine was right.

I bought and sold power often using power brokers in New York City. One of the brokers I did not use was Cantor Fitzgerald, who occupied many of the top floors in the World Trade Center. Almost all of the brokers at Cantor Fitzgerald were killed. One of the people I worked with at Seattle City Light with had interviewed for a job with Cantor Fitzgerald, but didn't get the job. She kept the plastic card that allowed access to the top floors of the World Trade Center building for only one day, the day of her interview. She showed me the card. The day of her interview was September 11, 2000. Exactly one year earlier.

The name of the broker I used most often was Michael. He had an amazing story from 9/11. His building was two blocks from the World Trade Center, and there was a plaza in front of his building. The police had set up barricades so that his building's plaza was the closest point anyone could get if they wanted to watch the World Trade Center burn. It had the best unobstructed view, and the plaza was packed. Meanwhile, he was in charge of the broker house, and nothing was getting done. Every call was someone asking if they were okay. He sent all of the other brokers home, and finally he decided to go home as well. He got to the street level and there were so many folks looking at the World Trade Center burning, that the only way for him to go was away from it. He got only about half a block and the building began to fall. Everyone ran, including him. He came to a set of stairs and went down them just as the rush of debris from the falling building flew past. Michael had gone down enough stairs so that the rush went over his head, but he turned around and saw the guy directly behind him who had gone down just two fewer stairs was bleeding badly from the back of his head. He started to try to help him when a policeman told him to leave as fast as he could. So he did.

Paul and Siriwan—Paul was a guy at SCL who was hired due to his knowledge of a certain software system we were using at the time. For about five years, Paul was the expert on that system and helped a great deal. Then, a decision was made to change software systems. Paul disagreed with this decision and refused to learn the new system. As a result, Paul went from being a valuable, helpful employee to doing what he called "research" that no one in management valued. At the City of Seattle, it turns out to be nearly impossible to fire someone who has five years of top scores in their annual reviews, especially since Paul's supervisor had changed. The new supervisor was trying to prove that Paul should be fired, with little success. As a result, Paul documented what he did every minute of the day.

It was only on the rare occasion that someone had a question on the old computer system that any of the other staff wanted to talk to Paul. Paul also had the unusual habit of staying at his desk for lunch, and his lunch was always popcorn.

My desk was near Paul's so I heard the following very calm, very polite exchange one day:

Siriwan (a co-worker) came by and said, "Paul, I have a question."

Paul calmly leaned forward in his chair, put the lid back on the popcorn tub, closed his desk drawer, clicked the timer on his watch and said, "Yes?"

Siriwan said, "I didn't realize you were at lunch, I can come back later."

Paul calmly clicked the timer on his watch, opened the drawer, pulled off the lid, grabbed some popcorn and leaned back in his chair.

Siriwan said, "But if you don't mind, I just have a quick question."

Paul calmly leaned forward in his chair, put the popcorn back, put the lid back on the popcorn tub, closed his desk drawer, clicked the timer on his watch and said, "Yes?"

Siriwan said, "I am sorry, your lunch is important. I can come back later."

Paul calmly clicked the timer on his watch, opened the drawer, pulled off the lid, grabbed some popcorn and leaned back in his chair.

Siriwan said, "But it will just take a minute."

This went on SEVEN TIMES. There eventually was an audience of about twelve people trying to stay quiet and not laugh by the time Siriwan— deadpan the entire time—finally did go back to her desk to wait.

Bunk Desks—There was a program at SCL where employees got paid a small amount if they made a suggestion that was implemented. The first time I "won" this award I just followed a certain request form to each person it was forwarded to, and asked them what they did with it before sending it on. I then pointed out that the form was being handled by nine people who checked it for errors, plus two more who *retyped it*. Sometimes just documenting the process can tell you how stupid it is.

One of the evaluators told me of a "bunk desks" suggestion to have two desks stacked together and every other employee would be given a tall tricycle to ride to their desk so that the employee on the tricycle would use the upper desk directly over the employee using the lower desk. For some reason, this suggestion was not implemented.

Diplomat?—I went with two other SCL employees to a conference in Portland, a woman named Sue and a man of Chinese decent I'll call "CV." CV was presenting, and the rest of us were just attending. I noticed that CV's suit looked extremely sharp and something like I would expect someone in the Chinese military to wear on a formal occasion. He looked like a diplomat.

After the conference, we were heading home. We were in a vehicle that had the city of Seattle logo on the doors. Sue was driving, I was in the front passenger seat and CV was in the back. We came up behind a police officer who was going the speed limit. Sue decided to pass. Both CV and I did not think this was a good idea and sure enough the officer pulled us over. The officer talked to Sue through my window on the right. I could not help but notice that he kept looking back at CV (who said nothing and stared straight ahead while the officer talked) and at the door decal. After one last glace at both the door and CV, the officer just asked Sue to please drive slower and went back to his car.

Pothole Studies—[TF] One of my most memorable experiences at Seattle City Light was being part of a river fish stranding study. This is a study to count the number of fish stranded by varying river flows. The amount of flow in a river below a dam is set by the water released through the dam, and the study was to find out the best way to release water to strand the fewest number of fish. (The answer, it turned out, is to "downramp"—that is, lower the river flows at night. This will strand the fewest fish).

Our job was to go from "pothole" to "pothole" and count the number of fish contained. A pothole is basically a big puddle formed when a river recedes. The pothole either dries out, or is refilled when the river level increases. If the pothole contains fish and it dries out, the fish die. Keith had designed this study (which became somewhat famous in the "fish stranding world") and was in charge of the entire study as well as the four of us "fish-counters": Me, Keith, Francis and Wayne. After carefully determining how deep the pothole was and how far it was from the river and the dam, Keith would "shock" it and the stunned fish would float to the surface for a few seconds. The other three would count the stunned fish quick before they recovered and swam away. I enjoyed the work, as it beat sitting in front of a computer all day.

Keith wore the contraption that shocked the potholes and the suit made him look like a cross between an astronaut and a deep sea diver. It had a 40 pound battery that was worn like a backpack, and electrodes extending about three feet from both arms along with "dead-man" switches that required both hands to hold the switches down in order to perform the shock. Francis was jealous and let everyone know he wanted to try the suit. All day long, Francis begged Keith to let him try the suit. Keith was unwavering: you are not trained, it is dangerous, etc.

Finally, after eight hours of shocking potholes without incident and eight hours of hearing Francis beg Keith to try it, we approached the last pothole. This one was circular, about twelve-foot diameter and about 18 inches deep. Keith relented. As Keith took off the gear and helped put it on Francis, Keith was carefully going over all the safety steps. Wayne and I could tell that Francis was excited and not listening. Finally, Keith was done with the safety training that Francis pretended to hear, and Francis was wearing the suit. On Francis, it looked even more like an astronaut than anything else. Ok, Keith said, are you ready? Francis said yes as he stood on the edge of the pothole. He took exactly one step forward, tripped, and fell face first into the pothole and completely disappeared under the shallow water.

Keith screamed "I knew this was a bad idea!" and flew into the pothole to pull him out.

Thirty minutes later, after Keith had shocked the pothole and he and uninjured Francis had counted all the fish without any help, Keith turned to Wayne and me and asked if we were ready to leave. We could not talk, much less stand up as we were still laughing so hard our stomachs hurt.

Bear Scare—When I was counting fish as part of a pothole study, a bear and I scared each other half to death. I am told bears can run 35 mph. I can verify that. I saw it myself.

I nearly died #5.

Bad Cow—When I was counting fish as part of a pothole study, we had to make our way from the road to each pothole alongside the river. Most of the time there was a short trail. One time, I had to walk across a fenced field that had cows in it. As I tromped across the field with my rubber boots and other equipment, the cows decided to follow me. Near the river, I stepped over the barbed-wire fence at a spot where it was about waist-high.

So did the cows.

When I got to the relatively small riverside sandbar that had the pothole, I was surrounded by cows. Keith, who was the head of the study, pulled up in a boat and said, "Hey, Rough, what is with the cows?" I started to tell him I didn't know when he suddenly started screaming and jumped out of the boat. He ran over and started hitting some cow with his clipboard that was eating the plastic pothole marker.

Bad cow!

Real Time—I was a Power Marketer at Seattle City Light. I bought and sold power and transmission all over the Western US. Mostly, the power and transmission dealings I did were for a month or more in the future. This was called "Month Ahead" in the lingo. If it was March, I might be buying or selling power to be delivered in the entire month of April, or May, or beyond. I was a Month Ahead trader.

Other people were the "Day Ahead" traders buying and selling power and transmission for the next day, and sometimes several days after that if a weekend was coming up. The Month Ahead and Day Ahead traders worked a normal 40-hour week, although since the power brokers were often in New York City, we tended to start early due to the time zones. I normally started at 7 am, and the Day Ahead folks usually started at 6 am or sometimes 5:30 am.

Then there were the folks, sometimes called "Hour Ahead" but more often "Real Time" traders. These folks kept the lights on 24/7. SCL used twelve-hour shifts, from six to six. All Real Timers had to eventually work both the day and the night shift. "Flipping" from day to night and back took some getting used to.

Power speculators might buy 25 MW of, say, June power in the Month Ahead market and then sell it day by day on the Day Ahead market, or even hour by hour in the Real Time market, hoping to be money ahead at the end of the month. I heard from a lot of people who made money this way (or the reverse, sell first and then buy it back). I suspect there were also those who lost money who just didn't call anyone to tell them about it.

It was decided that I should be trained as a Real Timer for six months, in order to better perform my job as a Month Ahead trader, especially since I was coming up with new deals that might impact the workload of the Real Timers. For most of the year 2000 I trained as a Real Timer. This happened to be the period called the "power crisis" with the highest electricity prices ever recorded, before or since. There was a bad drought in the NW, which meant that the NW was going to try to buy lots of power from California, rather than California buying from us, which was usually the case. Meanwhile, California had put in place a brand new "ISO" or Independent System Operator which was supposed to keep prices low, but in a drought situation, allowed prices to go quite high. Too high. Politicians in California were putting in place laws intended to deal with prices that were too high, but they had unintended consequences.

So, there I was at the Real Timer's desk, where you keep the lights on by making sure that you have exactly the right amount of power for the city of Seattle every four seconds. Everyone works on forecasts, which are never perfect. The Month Ahead forecast is used to buy and sell power such that if the Month Ahead forecast is perfect, there will be no need for Day Ahead trades. Of course, the Month Ahead forecast is always a bit off, so the Day Ahead forecast is made and the Day Ahead folks make needed trades. Occasionally, the Day Ahead forecast is quite accurate and nothing unforeseen happens, so the Real Timers don't have much to do.

Not on my shifts.

One thing that cannot be forecast is outages. If there is an outage within the city, perhaps caused by a tree falling on a power line, then people are not using power they planned to use—their lights are out—and we have power to sell. Balancing load and generation every four seconds is mostly automated for small changes, and it can be tough enough when folks are just randomly turning appliances on and off, but a major power outage can create a power surplus that needs to be sold or sometimes we have enough room behind our dams to hold back the water for later that we were going to use to generate the power. The decision to sell or hold back needs to be made quickly.

The flip side is that sometimes you have an outage of generating equipment or a transmission line. Now you might have to buy power in a hurry or generate extra power quickly.

Here is what happened to me on one of my Real Time shifts. When I got on shift, I was notified that California was having brownouts. They were 400 MW short. This meant there was not enough power for the entire West Coast, because California was offering to buy power at the maximum price allowed (for reference, the maximum price for "Real Time" power was about 5 to 10 times the rate the average homeowner was paying for power at the time). Because there was a drought, SCL's dams could not generate as much power as usual because there was less water than normal in the rivers. Same with the rest of the NW. Although we had less water than usual, we still had large hydroelectric plants that were generating a lot of power. Our Boundary dam, for example, was generating 700 MW of the about 1100 MW needed for the total power usage for the entire city of Seattle. If the dam had more water, it could have generated more, but 700 MW is still a lot of power.

We had a full Boundary dam outage. Very rare. The entire plant stopped generating. For a Real Timer, this is where you earn your pay and/or you crap your pants. Mr. Trainee had to find 700 MW—more than half of what was needed for the entire city and almost twice what California was short, and fast.

The power and load have to match every four seconds, but what happens automatically in an outage situation as "reserves" kick in, or what we call "leaning on the system." Essentially every plant anywhere in the NW is automatically required to temporarily kick in some MWs to keep the balance if there is a large outage. And this was a very large outage.

One way to think about it is that every plant that is "running" is asked to "sprint" for a while in an outage situation. That only works for a short time, like 20 minutes. After that you have a brownout, just like California. And just like California, it will be the top story on the local news because people's lives can be at risk. Not what a Real Timer wants. A Real Timer's Job One: Avoid brownouts.

I had 20 minutes to fix the Boundary outage imbalance problem or we would have brownouts. Power is usually sold in 25 MW increments, so 700 MW is a lot. And California was offering maximum price with no sellers. I was sweating. I found someone in Montana who was willing to sell to Seattle, but not to California. Technically not legal, but understandable, because at the time nearly all sales to California ended up in court as politicians were trying to claim price gouging. Meanwhile, NW utilities like Seattle just paid the big bucks and tried not to complain too much. We also found some utilities willing to swap power. The water that was going to be used behind our Boundary dam was still there. We had room behind the dam to store it thanks to the drought. Eventually the water SCL was planning to have Boundary generate with would be used to pay back the power swap once we got the plant working again. Plus, we had some plants on our system capable of generating more for a few hours.

Truth be told, somebody else at SCL found the swap power. I said "we" because I had to get extra help. Getting extra help is easy if you have a problem during day shift Monday through Friday. You just go grab one of the Day Ahead folks or a supervisor. I was lucky. At night and on weekends, you are by yourself.

So, it all worked out. We managed to find 700 MW in 20 minutes. No brownout. But I had to change my underwear. Different kind of brownout.

Ricochet—There is an electricity trading hub called the California/Oregon Border or COB. Power was traded there more often than any other place in the US when I was trading, at least partly because the rules changed for power going into California. Although power was traded at COB, no power actually stopped there. What would happen is that power would be sold on a Month Ahead basis at COB, for example 25 MW for the month of July. This means somebody promises to deliver 25 MW to COB for the entire month of July. Before July comes around, someone else will buy that power at COB and when the power actually flows it goes to a utility where it will be used for residential, commercial or industrial loads. The power never stops or stays at COB.

Because the rules changed for power going into California compared to power exiting California, there were two prices at COB, a northbound price, and a southbound price. It was almost always the case that the southbound price was higher. When pricing a deal at COB, you had to determine whether the power was northbound or southbound.

The other thing to realize is that power takes the path of least resistance no matter who owns that path. A utility may have ownership rights on a certain transmission line and no rights on the line next to it, so the contract says the power is travelling on the line where the utility has rights, but the power most often does not go where the contracts say it goes. In the power world, there sometimes is a big difference between what a contact says and where the power goes.

Because power goes wherever, there are rules against buying northbound COB power and just calling it southbound and collecting the difference between the two prices.

The only exception is a very special case called a ricochet. It is called a ricochet, because contractually the power goes from California all the way to a place north of California, such as Seattle, and then back into California instantly, thus legally turning northbound power into southbound power. In reality the power stays in California. I did only one ricochet in my 30 years at SCL. I did it in late 1999 just before the power crisis. It is rare to find the situation where it is legal. (Later, after the power crisis, we had federal regulators in our office who examined my ricochet deal and said it was legal.)

The legal situation is: First, where one utility in California wants to sell to another utility farther south in California and neither one is part of the Independent System Operator or ISO. Most Californian utilities are part of the ISO, but a handful, mostly small cities, are not. Second, the selling utility must have no contractual rights to transmission to the buying utility. Third, the only contractual path available to the selling utility is to COB. If all three are true, a ricochet is legal. Effectively it is a contractual deal where SCL does nothing but take ownership at COB northbound and instantly give back ownership at COB southbound and charge the difference in price. Pretty much collect a fee for nothing, but only entities north of California can do it.

I happened to be talking to someone from Enron one day just before the power crisis, and I explained how I had done a ricochet deal.

Next thing you know, Enron was doing them daily. Hmmm.

I guess I should say I am sorry for the power crisis?

Congratulations—Once per year there is a Western Systems Power Pool (WSPP) meeting for power traders. When I was trading, these meetings were not to be missed. All the power traders, who did their business over the phone, would meet and have fun. These WSPP meetings often involved golf, skiing or other fun activities. There was a "real" meeting which took about four hours (and was pretty boring), but it was always surrounded by several days and evenings of fun activities possibly including alcohol.

At a WSPP meeting in Calgary, I ran into a former auditor named Sherri who had audited SCL and then moved to Calgary. I dealt with auditors a lot because I was trading deals that nobody else did, so I had to write financial computer models to justify them. Then I had to explain my models and the deals to the auditors. Some of my more unusual deals were fascinating to the auditors. What auditors find fascinating other people might not. Just sayin'.

I had spent a couple of days with Sherri in an audit years ago and got to know her well. Years later at the WSPP meeting, Sherri told me she had been married for about a year and now was eight months pregnant. She was very bubbly and excited about her first baby arriving in just a few weeks. After chatting with her, I could not help but get caught up in her excitement.

I said goodbye to Sherri and then ran into a woman I had also worked with closely at SCL but I had not seen for about four years. She had been quite thin for the five years she had worked at SCL, and now appeared to be pregnant, so I said, "Congratulations!"

Idiot! I mentally scolded myself. I was caught up thinking about Sherri and forgot the number one rule: Never comment about a woman's pregnancy unless, as Dave Berry says, "you can see an actual baby emerging from her at that moment."

Sure enough. "For what?" She asked.

Amazing myself at my quick thinking, I said, "I thought I heard you got a promotion."

"I didn't think anyone knew about it yet. Thanks! "

YESSSSS! Save!

My Favorite Power Trade—My favorite power trade was a "double basis." A "basis" trade is where you trade power at one location for another.

SCL had a contract for a certain amount of power delivered to Boise, Idaho in a future month. Getting power from Boise to Seattle meant buying a transmission path. Actually, several transmission paths. Each company sells their transmission paths separately, so you have to buy in this case from three different companies, and then there are "losses."

When you transmit power over a line, not all of the power gets there. Some of the power is lost from heat. How much? The actual amount lost depends on a lot of things including weather, so rather than figure it out, each company just charges you a contractually set amount for losses. You put in 25 MW at one end, you get 25 MW at the other end, and you get charged for the fact that the other utility had to generate some amount so that you could have your entire 25 MW when you are done.

So, getting power from Boise to Seattle meant three transmission companies, and three loss charges. We had this contact for a long time, so the cost of transmission—a total of several hundred thousand dollars per month—was just part of getting the power to Seattle.

One time I found someone who wanted power delivered at Boise In a future month, and was willing to trade me power at the California/Oregon Border (COB) southbound. I said okay if you pay me (SCL) about $300,000. So I now had the same amount of power for delivery at COB southbound. COB southbound power is not good for Seattle as Seattle is north of COB, but bear with me. I then found someone who wanted COB southbound power and was willing to trade "Mid-Columbia" (or Mid-C, near Vantage, Washington) power for it. I said okay if you pay me about

$300,000. So now I had power for delivery in the same future month that was the same amount as the original Boise power, plus $600,000, but a big part of the benefit was that the transmission cost from Mid-C to SCL was less than one third of the transmission cost from Boise. So the total added value of this deal was close to a million dollars, *not including the value of the power*. This was my favorite of all the deals I did at SCL.

Management Priorities—I was a very successful power marketer by all measures. I was the only power marketer who was writing new contracts for types of trades we had never done before. Of the 13 power marketers at Seattle City Light, each was rated in six categories, and I was the top marketer by rating in all six categories. In 2008, which was a poor year for the US economy, I brought in $43 million in net new revenue for Seattle City Light. Late in the year, I was called into the office of my boss's boss. He told me that I had made more typos than any other power marketer. He was upset with my performance because accountants had to double-check the contracts I wrote and often found typos.

Wow. I thought I was on a prank show like Candid Camera. He was not amused when I pointed out that I was the only marketer writing new contracts and the other marketers were filling in the blanks in contract templates that I myself had written. Of course, I was making more typos than other marketers! No other marketers were writing new contracts!

In some companies, $43 million in net new revenue in a bad year (after accounting for typos, which didn't actually cost anything) would get you a bonus or some kind of increase in pay. At Seattle City Light it got me a scolding.

DAUGHTERS

Germs and our First Child—When we had our first child, by
coincidence we also bought a new car. In fact, we probably saved a bunch
of money by not adding any "extras" when we signed papers because my
wife was in labor. You can hurry car negotiations a lot by telling the
salesperson that your wife is in labor. When we got to the hospital, all the
"labor and delivery" rooms were full, so we had to go to a surgery room. I
wanted to record the event with a stand-alone camera on a mini-tripod,
but all the counters and tables were covered with obviously sterile tools. I
asked permission to film (back then it WAS film), and a nurse
unceremoniously used both (gloved) hands to grab all the tools off one
counter and toss them in the sink and say "you can put your camera
here." The lighting sure was great.

All went well, and I was handed my firstborn. I was awkward and
nervous, shaking a bit. She was cute and sleepy, but blinking at me (bright
lights) with fascination. We were moved into the surgery recovery room.
The instant we got there, my daughter pooped in the thin blanket. I had
never been a father before and had only held maybe three babies in my
life so I was extra nervous, (and you may remember my disaster at
babysitting) but even I knew that I needed a diaper. I looked around.
Since it was a surgery recovery room, there were no provisions for babies,
so no diapers. I saw a "nurse call" button and I pushed it.

All hell broke loose. Screaming alarms, flashing lights and about twelve
doctors and nurses accosted me and my wife beside me immediately.
What's wrong? They asked us both.

Weakly, I admitted that I could not find a diaper.

A large German-looking nurse grabbed me by the arm so hard it was
painful, pulled me aside and said venomously through gritted teeth, "If
you EVER need another DIAPER, DON'T push that button!" Got it. Roger.

Message received. Don't push the nurse call button in the surgery recovery room for a diaper.

After a quick stay in the hospital, we were on our way back home. Driving home, we were marveling about how our new daughter had not yet been exposed to real-world germs. She was born in a sterile surgery room, wearing all brand new clothes, riding in a new car seat in a brand new car.

When we got home and opened the car door to get her out, our beagle dog Sprough fixed that situation by jumping up and licking her entire face as well as anything else he could find, much to her delight.

Duck!—My daughter Amanda was in a university study from when she was newborn up to age one. According to the study, she was slightly behind average in physical development, but off the charts ahead in verbal development. She actually could talk before she could walk. Her cousin was three months younger, but could walk before she could. Meanwhile, she had about 2000 words at 12 months when the average kid had fewer than a dozen. She also had a stubborn streak, and would admonish other kids who mispronounced words.

Possibly one of the reasons she had so many words is that I would carry her around and point to things and state what they were. I remember when she was about 12 months, we were about to get on a ferry to cross Puget Sound, and were waiting for the ferry to load. I pointed to a seagull, turned to her and said, "Seagull." Amanda turned to me and said, "Duck."

"No," I said, "Seagull."

"DUCK!!" she said firmly and loudly, then turned away. That was the end of the discussion.

Building a House—Before we moved to Kirkland, Lorraine and I decided we were going to build a house. We found a builder who had a plan we liked. We found a lot we liked, and made some changes to the standard house design we had toured. We figured out how much we could afford, and this was going to be just barely affordable. Scary, because we had no leeway at all. But we signed papers, which meant by contract we knew how much it was going to cost.

A few months later, we went out and looked at the lot, and work had progressed well. We saw from the foundation that had been poured that the changes we had asked for had been made correctly.

A few days after we looked at the foundation, the builder called us into his office. Amanda was 18 months old at the time.

The builder told us that he needed an additional $7000 to finish the house. We didn't know what to say. There was absolutely no way. We didn't have an extra $70, much less $7000. The room was silent for about 15 seconds, then Amanda piped up and said, "God Dammit!"

We all cracked up. To this day, I don't know where she got that word. I had been very careful not to swear in front of her. I have a friend who still talks about the time I hit my thumb pounding a nail with toddler Amanda in earshot and I said "Bother!"

We walked from the contract and got our deposit back, since the builder had broken the contract at that point anyway. We ended up buying a house that had already been built, and we have been very happy.

At the time we signed the contract, our neighbor was the local Building Inspector Supervisor. He heard that we were having a house built, and said he would inspect it himself. I don't know whether us getting shafted by the builder had anything to do with it or not, but he condemned it. The builder ended up selling the condemned house for $30,000 less than our contract price. So rather than getting $7000 more, he got $30,000 less.

I am okay with that.

If a builder tries to screw you, it is nice to have a friend who is a Building Inspector Supervisor.

The house was condemned before it was completely finished. The builder ended up making changes to "our" plans to save money in finishing it, so the final house (still there!) is not quite what we "ordered."

A Lady—We were in a grocery store one day when two-year-old Amanda went up to a woman who was wearing a lot of makeup. She looked carefully at her then turned to Lorraine and me and in a loud voice said, "That's not a clown, that's a lady."

Loud Mike—I knew several guys named Mike. Amanda called them Neighbor Mike, Soccer Mike and Loud Mike. Loud Mike? Let's just say no matter how big the crowd is, you can always find my good friend Loud Mike. He saved seats for us once at a sold-out comedy film and we could hear him laugh the moment we entered the theater. He would have made a great politician. My offer to work on your campaign if you ever decide to run for something still holds, Mike.

Carolyn's Third Birthday—For sister Amanda's birthday in January, we invited ten kids, and twelve showed up. For Carolyn's third birthday on a sunny Saturday in July, we invited ten kids and none showed up. "Is it time for my birthday party?" she asked. "Not yet." We answered. Good thing she could not tell time. We waited two hours until some neighbors got back from the beach and grabbed them. Carolyn was happy. Whew!

In the Seattle area, nobody wants to be inside for a kid's birthday on a sunny Saturday in July.

First Day Skiing—Carolyn was our fearless one. When she was two years old, she wanted to go on a roller coaster. We found a kiddy coaster, the kind that is one loop and takes about one minute. My wife and I took her, and she loved it. When we got done, she wanted to go again. After about three times, my wife was done. Four more times and I was done, but Carolyn still wanted to go. We sat on a bench between the exit and the entrance, and Carolyn would come out of the exit, run over to us and say, "That's kinda fun. Do it again? OK!" and run to the entrance. She did this at least 25 times.

As I did with Amanda, I carried Carolyn around as a tot and pointed out things to try and increase her vocabulary. With Carolyn, however, I would occasionally point to something I knew she did not know to see what she would say. I pointed to our oven, knowing she had never heard the word "oven" and asked her what it was. She said it was a "Get-the-cookies-out."

We took her skiing for the first time, and I was a little worried about her fearlessness. She got off the chairlift and turned and headed pretty much straight downhill. Although this was a beginners chair, she still got going pretty fast. I followed and could barely keep up. She made it to the bottom and jumped right on the chair to go again. Once again at the top, she headed down as fast as she could go. This time, she crashed, sending up a plume of snow. I thought, oh, boy, here come the tears, and this might teach her to slow down. As I pulled up beside her, she got up and said "Phooey! Got snow in my mouth!" and headed downhill just as fast as before.

Track Dinner—One day our daughter Carolyn gave us 45 minutes notice that the track team—about 40 kids—was coming to our house for dinner. Sorry mom, didn't I tell you?

It turned out fine because they brought their own food and didn't mind sitting on the floor, but it certainly demonstrated how crazy our household was during the teen years.

Most of them sat on the floor because for some reason we could not find 40 chairs. In 45 minutes.

Lisa in the Hot Tub—Lisa, our third daughter, loved to watch. With two older sisters, there was always a "show" to watch.

We went to a water park one day, where they had a hot tub situated so that you could watch the action in the wave pool. We had our daughter Lisa with us in the hot tub when she was about three years old. The hot tub was one of those that seated about 12, and there were seats all around the edges. Lisa was standing on the seat between Lorraine and me. We were all watching Amanda and Carolyn in the wave pool. Lorraine and I looked away from Lisa for what seemed like 10 seconds to watch the wave pool, then turned around to find Lisa face down and floating motionless in the center of the hot tub.

YAHH!

Instantly I thrust her high into the air. She looked at me and calmly said, "Don't like that."

Me either.

Not Lisa—Lisa's real name is Elizabeth, but we have called her Lisa all her life. In one class in elementary school (fourth grade?), there was already a Lisa, so she decided to allow the teacher to call her Elizabeth, as that is what the official documents said anyway.

A new kid moved to town and invited about eight girls to a birthday party. At about 9 pm I went to get Lisa. The house was in an area that had few lights, and it was quite dark. I knocked on the door and the mom opened the door suspiciously, with the chain still attached and asked me what I wanted. I told her:

"I am here to pick up Lisa."

"There is no Lisa here!" she said and slammed the door.

I knocked again.

"I am here to pick up Elizabeth."

Taco Mints—Lorraine and I thought we were done having kids after three. Our daughters wanted another baby. They promised they would babysit. As it turns out, they did. In some ways our older three daughters talked us into having a fourth.

Tessa never seemed to want to leave when we went someplace she liked. She always wanted to stay "just a couple of minutes" which, when she was about 1 ½ years old, sounded like "taco mints." When we went to a Mexican restaurant, with Tessa, Carolyn and a friend of Carolyn's, Tessa didn't want to leave and Carolyn's friend looked at the menu for this new dessert item Tessa was talking about.

The older girls liked to have us drive past the street where we lived without turning in, because when we did that one-year-old Tessa's eyes would get big and in a concerned voice she would say "Home?"

The "Oops" Child—We like to ask people which of our children was the "oops" child. Amanda and Carolyn are three and a half years apart, Carolyn and Lisa two years apart, then Lisa and Tessa are seven and a half years apart. Most think it was Tessa due to the 7½ year gap, but actually Lisa was the oops child. We had always planned on a third child, but intended to have a three-year gap between Carolyn and Lisa because Lorraine wanted only one in diapers at a time. As noted above, Tessa was planned, partly by her sisters.

Oops and non-oops, we love them all just the same.

Perfect Soccer Game—I coached all four daughters in soccer. I was their coach when they were just starting out at the age of five playing three-a-side. The three-a-side teams usually had six players on the team. As the name implies, during games three girls would play at a time.

As girls got older, they would play more kids per game up to "normal" soccer at eleven-a-side. The teams would get need to get bigger as players got older, but normally there were not enough new signups, so teams would combine. I only wanted to coach one team at a time, so as each of my daughters turned five, I became the five-year-old's coach and let my older daughter's team get combined into another team or split between several teams.

When coaching soccer, what is a perfect game? With Tessa, my youngest, when she was playing three-a-side, I think her team had a perfect game. We won the game with a score of 6-0, and each player on Tessa's team scored one goal. If that is not a soccer coach's perfect game I don't know what is.

I coached all four daughters in soccer when they were young. This is Lisa's team, the "Dalmatians." That is our dumb dog *Jasmine*.

Teen Party—Lorraine and I went out of town and left our teen-aged kids at home. In general, you should not do this. When we came home, the house looked fine as we walked in, but the kids seemed nervous. We looked downstairs, and found a spot where our green carpet was black. In all their mad cleaning, they had missed this. Why was the carpet black? Mud. Our girls had had so many people over for a party while we were gone that the partygoers had tracked so much mud onto the entire carpet downstairs that it turned black. But they missed a spot when they cleaned up.

And, the trampoline was bent. It was a big sturdy 14-foot trampoline. How did they bend the trampoline? Don't ask a question if you don't want to hear the answer: if you get enough people to jump from the roof, you can bend a trampoline.

Daddy Warbucks—My daughter Lisa has always been interested in singing and acting. When Lisa was about to enter Juanita high school, they had the worst teacher I have ever seen as the singing (choir) teacher. It was not just my opinion. The drama teacher announced that there would be no musicals produced by the school that year (unlike previous years). It was the only time I have ever written to a school board and said please fire this teacher. They wrote back and said she had a two-year contract which would not be renewed. Sigh.

So, even though we live just a few blocks from Juanita High School, unlike all three of her sisters Lisa chose not to go there, but instead to go to Lake Washington High School (home of the purple kangaroos!). The choir teacher at LWHS was quite good, and that was very important to Lisa.

The drama teacher at LWHS decided on the musical "Annie" and tryouts were held. High school kids were given the parts for the adults, and they got elementary school kids to try out for the orphans. Lisa got "Lilly St. John" which was a decent part, and her sister Tessa, in elementary school, got one of the orphans. The theater was very nice, too, with some great sets and fun costumes. So, we had two daughters who were excited to be in this play.

Then came the bombshell. Not enough boys had tried out, so they could not do the play. The drama teacher was not willing to do the play with a female "Daddy Warbucks" so she sent out a note saying they had three days to find a male to play Daddy Warbucks or they would cancel the play, and thus probably not have a play that year. I had two very disappointed daughters.

So I said I would do it.

I had to sing.

I am not a bad singer. I am actually pretty good. I was in choir in high school.

I had to dance.

I am a bad dancer. Awful. Blame my *Shin Guards*. After many rehearsals the director decided to rewrite the play to remove all scenes where I danced! If the director goes through all the work of a rewrite, including all the notes for the lighting, orchestra, stage manager, etc., you know my dancing is bad!

Meanwhile at work I was being sent every week to Portland overnight, leaving Tuesday early morning, returning Wednesday late evening. This meant I missed two practices per week. Normally this would disqualify me, but they made an exception.

It all came together and I enjoyed myself. However, one night the girl who played my love interest in the play came over to our house and stole some liquor. This tested my acting skills. I had to act like I was in love with her on stage, when in fact I was pretty annoyed with her.

TRAVELS

The Second Mechanic—One Memorial Day weekend after I had been at Seattle City Light just over a year, I decided to go on vacation and visit SCL's Boundary dam. We were driving our full sized van, and had our newborn daughter Amanda with us. We planned to sleep in the van.

The area is very remote. The road to the dam is a 12 mile, dead-end road that is pretty much only traveled by people going to and from the dam. The speed limit is 50 mph, and I was going about that, when out of nowhere a deer ran in front of me. I could not stop in time, and I hit the deer with a big crash, sending it flying along with parts of the front end of my van. None of my family was injured.

My first thought was we were in big trouble. This was before cell phones (and even today the cell coverage in that area is poor). Although we were not injured, fluids were pouring out of the van and it was clearly not drivable. We were about three miles from Metaline, population maybe 50 or so, which is three miles from nowhere. The next town a few miles down the road also had a population of about 50. The nearest city, Spokane, was over two hours away. I wasn't even sure there was a gas station in the area, much less a car parts store. And this was a holiday weekend, so there were fewer workers at the dam. My first thought was that being on a long, dead-end road in a remote area on a holiday weekend was going to be a big problem.

I stood there for less than 30 seconds, when a small car drove up. The driver rolled down his window and speculated that we must have hit a deer. Yes, I admitted. "Well, there are two mechanics in town, one of them has gone fishing, but the other one can probably help you," said the driver. I didn't know what to say to that. He then said that his car was too small to tow my van, but he did have a tow chain, and he handed me a brand new unopened tow chain. I started for my wallet to pay the man, but he drove off. I watched him drive off in wonder.

Not 20 seconds later, a big truck drove up. The driver noted that we must have hit a deer. I said yes. He said, "Well, there are two mechanics in town, one of them has gone fishing, but the other one can probably help you." I started to say that I had heard that, when this driver interrupted and said he could tow my vehicle but he didn't have a tow chain. Suddenly he said, hey, that one will do just fine, and he grabbed the chain I had owned for all of 30 seconds, and started hooking his vehicle to mine. Another car pulled up. The driver said it looked like we hit a deer but we were being taken care of. He then said, "Well, there are two mechanics in town, one of them has gone fishing, but the other one can probably help you" and drove off.

Just then the police showed up.

My head was swimming at this point. Everything was happening so fast. The officer said it appeared that my vehicle had hit a deer and we should find the deer. We found it off to the side of the road, and it turned out to be pregnant and very dead. The officer then said he wanted to make sure the tow chain was hooked up properly, and as it happened the truck driver had just finished hooking up the vehicles. The officer inspected the work and approved. The officer then said, "Well, there are two mechanics in town, one of them has gone fishing, but the other one can probably help you." The wording was virtually identical in the four times that I had heard this, and I was starting to wonder if someone was pulling a prank or something. I chose not to question the officer.

With the officer leading the way, the truck towed our van to town. We stopped at a tavern, where there was a phone. Less than ten minutes had elapsed since we hit the deer! The officer suggested that I call my insurance company while they towed the van to the second mechanic's house which he pointed to from the tavern. The town was small enough that I could walk to my van once I was done with my call. I went inside the tavern and told the bartender that I had just hit a deer, and needed to use the phone to call my insurance agent. The bartender said, "Well, there are two mechanics in town, one of them has gone fishing, but the other one can probably help you." And then left to get the phone. Again, nearly identical wording! I got a very weird feeling about all this. Maybe it was adrenaline and stress, but I got kind of wound up and started to wonder what the heck I had gotten myself into.

Before the bartender came back with the phone, a patron walked into the bar. He noted that I was not from the area. I told him that I had hit a deer and was in the process of trying to call my insurance agent. The patron said (I swear!): "Well, there are two mechanics in town, one of them has gone fishing, but the other one can probably help you." At this point I almost exploded, "How the hell do you know he went fishing?" The patron's eyes got wide and he started to back away. "I saw him pulling his boat with his fishing gear heading out of town." He said, then backed out the door and almost ran away. I calmed down, and realized that these folks were just trying to help, even if they all talked the same.

After I called my insurance agent, I walked to the second mechanics house. By this time it was 6:45 pm on Saturday night on Memorial Day weekend. The second mechanic said to me, "I hope you don't mind, but I have tickets to a dance tonight and I would like to go. Would it be okay if I worked on your vehicle tomorrow?" "Fine. Great. No problem. Have fun." I said, amazed.

We had planned to cook dinner on a camp stove and sleep in the van anyway, so we did just that from where the van was. They were kind enough to allow us to use their bathroom before they left for the dance.

The following morning I stumbled out of the van at 9 am. I had to pee, and I was amazed that I had slept so long. "I am sorry to wake you up," said the second mechanic from the front of the vehicle. I told him that he didn't wake me up. Good, he said. He said he had tried to be quiet. Anyway, he was all done except he wanted me to turn the engine over. I did, and it was all fine. He asked for $50. I tried to pay him more, but that was all the cash I had, and he didn't want to fiddle with a credit card and we didn't have our checkbook. He was embarrassed that he didn't have the actual correct parts and had to improvise. However, he showed me how his improvised solution would get me at least 20,000 miles or more.

We were back on the road Sunday morning with virtually no lost time on our vacation.

So, if you ever hit a deer on a holiday weekend, be sure and do it somewhere near Metaline, WA, so you can get it fixed quickly and cheaply and get to talk to nice, helpful but repetitive people.

Caught a Big One While Fishing—I have never been a fisherman, but Lorraine's father invited me fishing, so I went. I caught a 200-pounder! That is, I got the fish hook stuck not only in my finger but in the bone of my finger, so we had to cut the trip short to go to an ER to have it removed.

Ross Lake—Ross dam is owned by SCL and as part of the computer modeling I was doing, I was very familiar with how the dam operated. I modeled the water levels behind the dam every day for many years. I also knew the lake has a bunch of floating cabins on it, and I knew those cabins were for rent.

One of the interesting things about the cabins on Ross Lake is you cannot drive directly there. You have four choices to get there: 1) you can hike about 4 miles to the cabins; 2) you can hike about ½ mile to the lake and have a boat take you across the lake to the cabins; 3) you can drive to Diablo Lake, take a boat across Diablo Lake, then a truck to Ross Lake, then a boat to the cabins (note, the dirt road the truck goes on goes only between the lakes); and 4) you can drive to the lake in British Columbia some 26 miles up the lake, then take a boat 26 miles to the cabins.

In 1981 when my daughter Amanda was six months old, we decided to rent a floating cabin on Ross Lake. It was a blast. We enjoyed it so much, we decided to go again the next year, with some friends Gil and Sherry. Gil and Sherry ended up getting divorced. Anyway, for whatever reason, we did not go to Ross Lake again for a few years.

One day at work, I was talking to Kathy, a student intern who sat next to me. She said she had a reservation to stay at some cabins that cancelled. I suggested that she see if she could rent cabins at Ross Lake. She did and she loved it.

The following year Kathy went again, only this time she invited my family along. We have been going with her ever since. Each time anyone checks out, they reserve the same cabin and time for the following year. As a result we see the same people every year. We have become good friends with many of the people who rent the other cabins every year. We are up to 27 years and counting.

For many years we were in a cabin that slept ten, and as my family grew, occasionally friends were added and Kathy's family grew, too, we needed more room. So every year we would put our names on the list of folks who wanted to rent an additional cabin, in case someone did not sign up to rent the following year. Every year we were unable to rent an additional cabin until after a decade or so, one year someone died and we got to rent their cabin.

Ross Lake is fun, but someone has to die to rent a cabin there these days.

At Ross Lake. Lorraine, Amanda, Carolyn, Lisa, Tessa.

Exchanging Houses in Europe—We exchanged houses to go
on vacation in Europe several times. When you have a large family, it
makes a lot of sense. We swapped houses and cars, and were able to
have toys in the back yard for the kids, etc.

Our first exchanges were with a family in Amsterdam for three weeks
followed by a family in southern France near Nice for a little over two
weeks. We got an over-enthusiastic taxi driver in Amsterdam who could
not quite fit all five of us including our luggage into his vehicle, so we

ended up losing some luggage along the way as the trunk did not latch. We got it back.

Welcome to Europe! Should we go back and get your luggage out of the street now?

The neighbors across the street in Amsterdam came to welcome us on the first day. They were nice people and like nearly all the Dutch, they spoke English quite well, (although the woman did offer to "sit on our babies" one night—I think she meant babysit). They were replacing the floors in the house across the street. He said that his family had owned the house for over 500 years and "we always replace the floor every 100 years." I think he was serious. They brought over Dutch vegetarian lasagna for us the first night. Due to the Dutch cheeses and vegetables that we had never seen, it was unlike anything we had ever tasted. Lisa, my three-year old, was asked if she liked the lasagna. Her reply: "I love chicken!" One year later these folks wrote us and told us that if they ever went to a restaurant and did not like the food, they would look at each other and say, "I love chicken!"

I had mentioned that I played soccer in a letter to the Amsterdam folks, so they signed me up for a soccer team. What fun! At the time the soccer fields in the Seattle area had parking lots with nice landscaping but the fields were dirt. Meanwhile, in Amsterdam the parking lots were dirt but the fields looked like landscaped golf course putting greens. I think Amsterdam had their priorities correct. There were about six fields in the park where we played. One of the players on my team complained that we had the "crummy field" because one very small section of the field had brown grass. Hey buddy, we play on dirt and you complain that some of your grass is not green enough? All games ended at the same time, and when the games were over a restaurant opened up just for the players (all men's teams), with beer and wine available. There were 12 tables, each large enough to hold one team. It was very well done. I was the only one who did not shower and change before dinner at the restaurant, because I did not expect showers to be available. One of my teammates noticed, and asked if my wife liked me coming home after a game all sweaty and smelly. I told him she is used to it.

The Berlin Wall had just come down, and so we wanted to drive to Berlin. I found out that the exchange car we had available to us could go exactly 92 mph maximum. On the autobahn, I went to Berlin with the pedal all the way to the floor pretty much the whole way. I dared not get in the left lane, as many cars were going much faster there. When we got to Berlin, I went into a public restroom. It was free to pee, but it cost the equivalent of 35 cents to wash your hands. The sinks looked as though they had never been used! Imagine asking men to pay to wash their hands after peeing!

We needed a place to stay for one night in Berlin. I went to a place where they arranged hotel rooms for tourists. The line was pretty long. A man standing near the line who said his name was Mr. Elsner asked me if I needed accommodations and was okay with staying in a private apartment. I said yes and I was, but there were five of us including three children. No problem, said Mr. Elsner. We then left, and I followed him to his one-bedroom apartment. I didn't know how this was going to work, but it did. My wife and I slept in his bed and our three kids slept on blow-up mattresses on the floor while Mr. Elsner slept on the sofa in his living room. He made us breakfast in the morning and it was quite good. We all enjoyed our stay with Mr. Elsner. Whenever I said "thank you" to Mr. Elsner, he always said "please." I think it was because in German the word "bitte" means both "please" and "you're welcome."

When leaving Amsterdam, we had to rent a car, because although we had exchange use of cars in Amsterdam and in Nice, we could not take a car from one to the other. I called all over Amsterdam and could not find a price as good as my travel agent at home had mentioned before we left, so I ended up calling Seattle to get our travel agent to book us a car in Amsterdam.

We drove first to the black forest and stayed one night there. Then we went to Friedrichshafen, where we paid a small fee to get a reservation at a hotel in town, then went to dinner. After dinner, when we went to the hotel, they had given our room away because we did not show up right away. I told them we had paid a fee, but they didn't know anything about that. They called around, and there were no more rooms anywhere in town or even in the neighboring towns. We ended up driving late into the night and spending the night in the car in Vaduz, Liechtenstein (a tiny country between Austria and Switzerland). We were bummed and the kids were cranky. We then went to a hotel in Brig, Switzerland and I not only checked in, but I made sure I had the key in my hand. We wanted to see the Matterhorn near Zermat, which involves a train ride and a hike. The hike takes you about a mile into the woods, where we came upon a sign saying that going over a bridge would cost about $1 per person. But there was just the sign on the trail, no place to pay, no building, no person. I looked back to Lorraine and the kids who had not caught up yet, then turned around and there was a small man, less than 5 foot tall, with his hand out. I still do not know where he came from (or went afterwards), but he wanted to be paid for the bridge crossing. (Trip, trap, from the Billy Goats Gruff story started playing in my head).

We got back about 10:45 pm, and the hotel was dark. I thought, no problem I have the key. Turned out that the key was to the room, but not the front door of the hotel, which was locked. The kids started to cry— they did not want to sleep in the car again. I ended up finding out which window was the owner's window and threw rocks at it to wake him up, so that we could get into the hotel. The owner was mad at me for waking him up, but I think they should have keys that work for the front door of the hotel AND the room. To cater to obnoxious American tourists, for example.

The people we exchanged with in France lived in Marseille, but had a summer house in Cagne Sur Mer, near Nice. We went to the summer house first. The car we exchanged to drive was a Volkswagen Golf, except that there were two headlight switches. The second headlight switch turned on the radio. That was a bit strange, since we could not adjust the volume or change the radio station. Just on or off. Odd, but otherwise, it was fine. Three days later we were driving on a bumpy road and the entire dashboard fell away, revealing a very fancy radio, CD player, etc—a favorite for thieves. It was well hidden!

In San Tropez we found a small restaurant. Not speaking French, we guessed at what five-course meals to order. As luck would have it, everything I ordered was wonderful, and everything Lorraine ordered was awful. I noticed that the entire restaurant was tables, and there was no kitchen. I started to wonder aloud where the kitchen was, when I looked up and said, "Aha! They have a dumbwaiter." My daughter Amanda shushed me, "Dad! That is not nice!"

I had a super-telephoto lens with me, which was handy for beaches in San Tropez.

The problem with high school French, Lorraine discovered, is that when you ask for directions, you get them! "I think he pointed that way, but I didn't understand anything else."

One Sunday, we went to Marseille and we decided to visit the Chataeu d'If, an island near Marseille where the Count of Monte Cristo supposedly was held prisoner, according to the book by Alexander Dumas. We did not have quite enough francs to get all of us on the boat, but the boat operator allowed us to board for all the francs we had. When we got to the island, it is just a big rock—no vegetation at all—and the only thing on the island is the old prison now turned into a museum. It cost 2 francs to get in. We had no more francs! Did they take credit cards? No. American cash? No. Was there an ATM on the island? No. It looked bleak. The boat returned in two hours, and it looked as though all we could do was wait for it. The museum attendant finally let us in free.

Interesting tour of the museum, and I had not read the book. When we got back to Marseille, a newspaper reporter stopped us and asked us how we liked the tour. We did not speak French, but the photographer translated. We ended up getting a big article in the Marseille newspaper the next day. Our 80-year-old neighbors in Marseille complained that they had lived in Marseille their entire lives and had never been in the paper, but these damn Americans were here for only three days and they get a big article! I am told (I don't speak French) that in the article I claim to have memorized the book.

After six weeks of living in one exchange house or another, we spent a night in Paris at a hotel. We tried to cook our own food as we had become accustomed, but there was no way to cook at the hotel and no nearby markets or stores to buy food. We were forced to eat at a restaurant!

When we got back from six weeks in Europe, I asked my six-year-old daughter Carolyn what was her favorite part of the trip. She said the shuttle train at SeaTac airport.

Second Trip to Europe—We traded houses with a family from York, England and did a time-share trade in Spain for our second trip to Europe. In order to trade houses, we wrote letters to many people. A certain family near Peterborough wanted to trade with us, but we insisted on a car that could hold all six of us, which they did not have. These folks asked if we could stop by and stay at their house on the way to York, as they were about half way from London to York. We thought that would be fun. We got into the train station at 11:30 pm, which did not bother them. They had to bring two cars to take us from the train station to their house, and they did not mind. I rode with the woman. I could not help but notice that she was driving about 95 mph on dark one-lane roads at about midnight. When we got there, her husband said, "What took you so long?" These people had three daughters that were almost exactly the same ages as our three oldest daughters. It was a major highlight of our trip to have these six girls make fun of each others' accents. I enjoyed having my accent ridiculed. "Let's take the caRRRRR, and go to the maLLLLL then play socceRRRRRR," they said. Meanwhile, my girls were doing their best to exaggerate their hosts' English accents as well.

When we got to York, there was a neighbor who showed us the town. He told us where to park, and we enjoyed our tours. However, when we got back to the car, it had been broken into. Nothing was stolen, but an empty camera bag was lying on the ground near the car. I guess the would-be thieves thought there was something in that bag. We called a window repair place to get the car window fixed, and the guy on the phone said, "don't worry, we'll oover it for you." What? What do you mean "oover?" I finally had him spell it. "H-o-o-v-e-r" was what he spelled, as in the name of a vacuum cleaner company. Apparently a verb meaning vacuum. I didn't know.

We drove into Scotland, and went to Crathes castle, very spooky looking. It seemed haunted because the place looked so scary. The spiral stone stairs upward were dimly lit—the only light coming from thin windows that were used for archers to defend the castle. I was getting spooked. I kept thinking what a great place this would be for a horror movie. I looked at the stone steps winding up toward the next floor. There was a thump. It was dark, but I swear I saw blood dripping down the stairs. Yes, it was blood! Dripping down the stairs. I got really spooked now. Then I heard it—the ambulance. The woman in front of me had fallen backwards and cracked open her head. That was her blood!

When we were ready to leave England, I found out the bus we needed, and we went out to a nearby bus stop. We had plenty of time. Bus after bus went by our stop without stopping. We started to worry. Finally, I walked out to the middle of the street and forced the next bus to stop. He told us that no bus stopped at the stop we were at, and told us where to go for a bus to actually stop, but did not let us board his bus. We ended up making our flight, but were the very last to board.

In Spain, the company we rented our car from online didn't mention that we needed to pick it up at another company's rental desk. We asked where the desk for the company we rented from was and were told that they did not have a rental desk. That was a problem we didn't need. Something to note if you ever rent online from a company in Spain: Where do you pick up the car?

We had two timeshare trades on the Southern Coast of Spain, one week in Fuengirola and one week in Marbella. In Fuengirola we got somehow upgraded to the nicest unit in the place, with a 180 degree view. Spoiled! It seemed like very few Americans vacation in Spain, although of all the 22 countries I have visited, I think I would choose Spain as a place I would like to go back to before most other countries. I am a Spain fan.

We found some folks from Idaho who had two daughters who also played soccer like all four of our girls. The six girls found some local Spanish boys who had never heard of girls playing soccer. Soon, they were treated to a girls' team beating a boys' team.

We took a tour boat to Morocco. While walking around in Morocco, those on the tour had to wear a badge to identify themselves as tour participants. That badge might just as well have said "Please pester me with your overpriced trinkets! Stick them in my face as I walk along and continue talking and pestering me no matter what I say or do!" I have only been to Morocco once, but based on that I would advise you to have some kind of personal protection, such as mace or even a water bottle to pour on these irritants. Screaming, running, and ignoring did nothing to deter these trinket-selling pests. The police were no help at all, if anything they seemed to be waiting for a tourist to punch one and then arrest the tourist. My suggestion based on a sample of one visit is skip Morocco completely. I enjoyed the architecture and history more in Spain than in Morocco. Everything I saw for sale was available in higher quality in Spain at about the same price. If you decide to go, refuse to wear anything that identifies you as a tourist, and don't say I didn't warn you.

Estes Park Lunch—We vacationed in a resort on the west side of Rocky Mountain National Park for a week one July. While we were there, we made plans to have a picnic lunch in Estes Park, on the east side of the park with some friends who would meet us there. Getting to Estes Park from our resort meant driving on Trail Ridge Road, the highest paved road in the country, reaching heights of over 12,000 feet above sea level. Since the road is way above the tree line, as we headed east we could see for miles. It was sunny, warm, a bit dusty and blue skies in most directions, but behind us to the west we saw some ominous, very dark clouds, and they seemed to be getting closer. As we got past the continental divide over 10,000 feet, we could tell the nearly black clouds were definitely heading our way. They didn't reach us until just as we got to Estes Park, and what a downpour! It rained so hard it was difficult to even get out of the car, much less have a picnic. Darn! We thought that mid-July would be a good time for a picnic, but no. We ended up leaving all our picnic stuff in the car and going to a restaurant with our friends. The pouring rain kept us (and just about everyone) in the restaurant for nearly three hours. Finally, the clouds passed, it got sunny again, and we said goodbye to our friends.

We started back to our resort the way we came, but soon came upon a sign. The sign said Trail Ridge Road—the dusty road we had just travelled—was closed due to twelve-foot drifts of snow.

Gathering All Doug Roughs—Someone sold me a "Book of Roughs" one day. In it were the names of supposedly all the people in the world with the last name "Rough." I knew the name was uncommon. My sister once looked in the New York City phone book and found only one "Rough"—her. This "Book of Roughs" had maybe two thousand names, and every one of the people I knew with the last name Rough was listed with the correct address and phone. Maybe it did have all the Roughs.

One day I noticed that there were exactly seven Doug or Douglas Roughs in the "Book of Roughs." Of the seven, one was me, one in Ohio, Toronto, London and the other three in Scotland. Since I was planning to visit Scotland in a year, I decided to see if I could get all seven of us to meet in Scotland in a year. I contacted them all. It sounded like it might happen! The Ohio Doug was in the US Air Force, and could go pretty much anywhere free. The Toronto Doug owned a big company and said visiting Scotland might be fun and would plan on it. The London Doug worked for the airline industry and was up for it. The three Dougs in Scotland were non-committal, but we thought we could talk them into it. A local radio station even interviewed me on the unusual planned gathering.

As the day approached, it all started to unravel. The Ohio Doug said he was sorry, but his wife was due with his first child that day. The Toronto Doug said he had some kind of shareholder revolt he had to deal with. Two of the Dougs in Scotland said that they didn't want to drive that far (20 minutes and 35 minutes!) in the rain, and the other Scottish Doug didn't answer his phone. The only Doug that showed up besides me was the London Doug, but he was great fun. I gave him one of my old nameplates from my desk at work, and invited him to the US for the next Thanksgiving.

Doug Roughs

Buses in Ecuador—My daughter Amanda went to Ecuador for six months as part of her college education. We decided to visit her. Things are different in Ecuador. Buses, for example, are owned by individuals, and the cost of a bus ride was very cheap when we were there at 15 cents for local rides. The US dollar was the official currency, so there was no "exchange rate." To make the most money, the bus driver picked up and dropped off as many passengers as possible. To speed up this process, they stop for women and children, but just slow down for able-bodied men. Men were expected to grab the bus as it went by and climb aboard. Men jumped from the moving bus to depart. We saw a lot of face plants. I was glad to be with my wife and daughter. The bus stopped for them.

In Spanish, "bathrooms" are "cuartos de baños" meaning "rooms of baths" often shortened to "baños" which means "baths." Meanwhile, in Ecuador there is a resort town built around hot springs. The name of that town is "Baños" again meaning "baths." If you go to the bus station in Ecuador and follow signs for "Baños" you might find yourself on a bus to a resort town or you might find yourself in a room with toilets. We found ourselves in this predicament as we took a bus to the resort town of "Baños."

At one point on our bus trip, I was looking ahead at the two-lane highway our bus was traveling on. About a quarter-mile ahead, I saw a car coming toward us downhill in our lane passing a slower vehicle. The car in front of our bus decided at this moment to pass the car in front of it. Uphill.

Idiot! I immediately thought, as there clearly was not enough room for four cars on the two lane road at speeds of over 60 mph. Did I mention that this was a mountain road with no guard rails and one side had at least a 50-foot drop-off?

Anyway, I didn't get much of a chance to think about the car in front of us being an idiot before our bus driver decided to pass the car in front of us who was passing the car in front of it. Uphill.

167

What!!??!! No way was there room for five vehicles! I was suddenly very unhappy to be in the front seat of this bus!

In the end the car going downhill being passed skidded into the shoulder, while the car passing downhill made it barely around that car and as far onto the shoulder as he would fit, still leaving a little over half of both cars in the road. Something similar happened on the uphill side, the bus straddled the middle and all five vehicles missed colliding by about one to two inches each. None of the vehicles plunged off the unprotected cliff.

At least four other people on my bus gasped besides me, meaning that this must have been a dangerous move even by Ecuadorian bus driving standards.

Breakfast in Baños—We had an interesting breakfast in Baños, the resort town in Ecuador built around some natural hot springs. The restaurant had a patio in front with tables, and since it was a nice morning, we chose to sit outside. The cost for one cooked egg, toast, a muffin, a pastry, some fruit, fresh orange juice and coffee was $1.30. Again, Ecuador uses US currency, so this was exactly the cost including tax and tip. After taking our order, rather than going back into the restaurant with the order, the waitress instead crossed the street to the small market there. Moments later she passed us on her way to the kitchen carrying a small bag.

The ultimate just-in-time inventory technique. Don't buy food until the customer orders it.

Urchins on the Wheel—While in the resort town of Baños we saw a Ferris Wheel. It was powered by what looked like a 1970s Chevy with the exterior and tires removed. Someone sat in the driver's seat, and started the "car." A set of pulleys attached to the engine then caused the Ferris Wheel to turn. It was a kick. There were three of us, my wife, my

daughter and me. The cost was $1 each, which was expensive by Ecuadorian standards, but we did it anyway. No one else was around, so it looked like the three of us in one seat would be it for the ride.

Once the "car" was started, out of nowhere a bunch of children appeared. They all carefully climbed on without assistance. We went three times around and the entire Ferris Wheel was full, all children except for us. We were the only ones the assistant helped on and off. Aside from the safety considerations, I enjoyed the fact that we gave all those urchins a ride.

The Most Dangerous Road in the World—My vote for the most dangerous road in the world is the road heading east from the town of Baños toward the Amazon jungle in Ecuador. Here is what we found about 15 years ago when we took this road.

First, it is a one-lane dirt road with no guard rails and a huge canyon on the north side (as you head east downhill, on your right). The first thing you see as you leave touristy Baños is a zip line across the 200-foot deep canyon. We did not try the zip line. Although it is a one-lane road, there are other vehicles, trucks and the occasional bus that need to pass going in the opposite direction. Going downhill, passing an uphill vehicle means going to the right to the unprotected edge to let the other vehicle pass. When we were letting a bus pass, I saw part of one of our tires briefly over the edge, nothing below it for about 200 feet. There are big ruts and the driver said he learned "the hard way" to avoid puddles, so any driving around road hazards typically put the vehicle nearer the edge.

We had to travel directly through a waterfall. No way around it, and you needed to go quickly or you risked the jeep getting washed with all the water splashing sideways off the cliff. It was about 20 feet of driving through a large amount of water that was landing on the car and then washing directly off the edge of the road.

Next up were a few small bridges, over small tributary creeks, with only a 10 foot drop or so. These bridges were a single solid slab of metal eight feet wide without edges. (By comparison, a standard parking spot is nine feet wide. These bridges made parking slots seem wide!). This means our six-foot-wide jeep had to drive straight over these bridges with only a one-foot leeway on each side. After the bridge, giant cracks in the road to drive over where rocks that fell into the cracks ended up in the river far below. Next was a quarter-mile long single-lane tunnel, with no lights of course. We met a bus half-way in and had to back out of the pitch-black tunnel to let them by with only our dust-covered backup lights to guide us. Later, we had to stop to roll a two-foot diameter rock from the middle of the road off the edge of the road into the canyon below in order to pass. Since we had passed an uphill bus only five minutes before (our tunnel bus), either the rock fell *after* the bus passed, or *because* the bus passed.

Up to that point I hadn't worried about the possibility of rocks knocking us off the road. Thanks, rock.

After that, more ruts and more vehicles to squeeze past. Obviously we were white-knuckled the entire way, but you start getting used to the craziness after a while. After about eight miles of this we started to calm down. Then, the driver turned to me and said, "This next part is very dangerous!"

Huh?!? Compared to what?

It turned out that we were approaching a 90-degree turn. The driver said there were more vehicles at the base of the cliff near the 90-degree turn than anywhere else on the road. The reason is that drivers get complacent by this point, and start driving 25 mph or more, even though the road is dangerous. It is not possible to see around the corner and not possible for two vehicles to pass here, so if two vehicles meet at the corner and one or both are going more than about 5 mph, they will both go over the cliff. And many have.

So anyway, we lived. Barely. Not a good drive for a stress-free vacation.

Flying to Puerto Jimenez, Costa Rica—One of our crazy
adventure vacations where we traded houses was in Costa Rica, near
Puerto Jimenez. This is a tiny town where the only paved road is the
runway for the airstrip. The flight to get there involved flying from Seattle
to LAX, then to Guatamala City then to San Jose, Costa Rica all by large
commercial airliner. Once in San Jose, the capital of Costa Rica, we
needed to change airports to fly to Puerto Jimenez. We took a taxi from
the large airport to a much smaller airport, where the only building, the
terminal, was about half the size of your average 7-11 store. Our flight
was supposed to leave at 3:30 pm, but that time came and went. Finally,
at about 3:45 someone came up to me and told me something that I think
was supposed to comfort me, but only made me nervous, "Mr. Rough, I
am sorry but we cannot start our plane. But don't worry, we are renting
another plane." I suddenly realized we were in a small Central American
country and wondered if they were renting from "Jose's fruit stand and
plane rentals."

The normal plane that they could not start seated 25 people. On this
flight, because they had only six customers, they rented a plane that
seated six. There was my wife and two of our daughters, plus another
couple. I was seated facing a woman I did not know.

It took a while to fit all the luggage and people in such that the small
plane was properly balanced. Once that was done by the pilot (of course),
he climbed aboard. He tried to start the engine and it coughed and
sputtered out. He tried again, with the same result. The third time, same.
The fourth time the engine caught, and we immediately started moving
and the plane jumped into the air after only a few feet of runway rather
suddenly. The woman sitting across from me started screaming at the top
of her lungs. The higher and higher we rose, the louder this woman
screamed. She was obviously terrified and clutching her seat. As we
approached the mountain range we had to go over, we hit some

turbulence, and her screams somehow got worse. The little plane got tossed around pretty badly by the turbulence. Finally, we got past the mountain range and approached the airport. Her screams continued. She finally stopped screaming after we touched down safely. She didn't say anything to us as we got off the plane, but she didn't help us have a nice flight, that was for sure.

There were no buildings of any kind at this airport. The only pavement was the airstrip. Off in the distance, I saw a man on a bicycle approach and stop next to the plane. He had a clipboard, and was happy that our names were on his sheet of paper. He checked us off, and pedaled away.

We were met by the man whose house we would be trading our house for. His family was staying at our house, and we were staying at his house. For some reason, he could not join his family on vacation. We climbed into his Jeep for the 12 mile trip on dirt roads to his house. About half way there, he ran out of gas. He didn't seem worried in the slightest. I know this guy, he said, nodding at the house his Jeep had stalled in front of. Without going to the house, he went into the detached garage, and came out driving a different Jeep. We transferred our stuff into this Jeep and continued on our way. We had to ford a small stream at one point, so I can see why everyone had a Jeep.

The house was like a normal two story house like you might see anywhere in the US, except it had no exterior walls. Birds and bats could and did fly through the living room. It took some getting used to. The house was on 58 acres, so there were no neighbors nearby, and the plants were so thick that wind was not an issue. It rained a lot, but the rain came straight down, and did not splash into the house.

My daughter Lisa was coming a day later. She called on the phone before she came and asked how our flight to Puerto Jimenez was. We said, "Fine."

After Lisa arrived, she said that she saw dolphins swimming in the ocean below her from the 25-seater plane she flew in on. Did we see the dolphins? No, we missed that, for some reason.

Climbing Mount Rainier—If you are raised in the Seattle area, and are "outdoorsy" at all, climbing Mount Rainier is probably on your bucket list of things to do before you die. My friend Dan had climbed it and asked me if I wanted him to take me up someday. Heck yes, I said. Lorraine overheard and said she wanted to go, too. So we made plans.

At the time, 75% to 80% of attempts to climb Rainier did not make it. The weather was too unpredictable. You needed serious climbing gear—ice axe, crampons (spikes for the bottom of your boots to stick to ice), ropes, etc. We didn't have all that but my sister did, and we borrowed from my sister Linda and her husband. She (and others) said never borrow or lend ropes, so we bought our own ropes. You also need practice, especially for "ice axe arrest" which means stopping yourself on a steep slope using your ice axe if you fall. We spent one Saturday on the lower part of the Mountain tossing ourselves backwards off a steep slope for several hours to learn the arrest technique. When the slope is only twenty feet or so and ends in a big pile of soft snow like our practice area did, it was fun. Higher on the mountain, there were 2000-foot slopes that have nothing soft at the end.

There are two main climbing routes on Mount Rainier, the Camp Muir route, which is faster but steeper, or the Camp Sherman route, which takes several days. We chose the Muir route. You start from the aptly-named small town of Paradise, at about 5400 feet of elevation, where you park. Beautiful place, Paradise. This was July, and the wild flowers were in bloom, but still lots of snow around. The first leg of the climb is to hike to Camp Muir at the 10,000-foot level. This is steep, but regular hiking, albeit mostly on snow. You tend to be wondering why you have an ice axe, ropes and crampons (in your pack at this point). As climbers do, we spent the night at Camp Muir.

Starting to climb time at Camp Muir is 3 am. Very dark. Why? Because you want to climb on solid ice. Later in the day the ice and snow starts to melt and it can be difficult and much more dangerous. So we planned to start from Muir at 3 am. In reality I think we were the last group to leave (about six groups that day) at 3:20 am.

Our group was: Dan, Lorraine and me, plus two of Dan's friends. Before we left, we were instructed to put the crampons on and rope our group of five together. Just a few hundred feet beyond Muir, you find out why. A very steep icy slope of about 2000 feet. We were roped together so that four people digging crampons and ice axes into the snow and ice could stop a completely unconscious person sliding off a cliff if necessary.

Right away we saw a huge thunder and lightning storm coming toward us! Fortunately, the top of the clouds were about two thousand feet below us. It was thrilling to watch a thunder and lightning storm pass by "underneath" you while watching it from above. At night! Someone's flashlight was strong enough to light up part of the top of those dark clouds, too. Each lightning flash lit up a different part of the night landscape plus part of the mountain. Incredible. The clouds were moving quite fast, too, which we didn't think about at the time.

Just past "Dead Man Flats"—where twenty people had died in a bad avalanche one year—as we approached Disappointment Cleaver (after hearing some of these names, you wonder what you have gotten yourself into), we ran into a large group turning around. It was being led by the legendary Lou Whittaker. He is well-known as *the* most experienced climber of Mount Rainier (and one of the founders of REI), and I was honored to meet him on Mount Rainier. He was turning around with his group because winds at the top were 75 mph.

Uh-oh.

If expert climber Lou Whittaker is turning around....

Lou took us aside and said he was leading a group of "bankers and accountants" and was just being extra careful with an inexperienced group. He said if we were in good shape and thought we could handle 75 mph winds at the top, we should go ahead. Hmmm. We paused, talked about it, and decided to keep going.

Only one group can go up or down Disappointment Cleaver at a time. We had to stop, because the group ahead of us was *coming down*. As they got to the bottom we asked them why they were quitting. They were spooked by the 75 mph winds Lou had mentioned. At this point, one of Dan's friends said he no longer wanted to go. At the same time one of the group of five that had just come down the Cleaver said he still wanted to go up but got outvoted. So we switched, and I got roped to the guy we switched with, and I never saw Dan's friend again (not that he died or anything, I just never saw him again).

So, up we went. After Disappointment Cleaver—where you are climbing straight up with hands and feet (and thankful for the crampons)—most of the way was trudging along on ice or icy rocks.

The thin air starts to be an issue. While none of us felt the air at Muir was terribly thin, as we got to the 11,000 foot level it got so we all had to pause once in a while to catch our breath. At the 12,000 foot level, we were pausing much more often. At 13,000 foot, we were pausing about every 3-4 steps. At the 14,000 foot level, we were pausing every single step. Fortunately, the mountain is 14,410 feet, so we only had 400 feet of pausing every step. (I cannot imagine how much pausing climbing Everest at 29,000 feet would take).

When you are all roped up, you go at the pace of the slowest climber.

We were on glaciers much of the way. Glaciers move slowly down mountains, and they tend to have cracks in the top as they go over boulders and such. These cracks can be quite deep, and you don't want to fall in them, as getting out is a major problem. Plus you might die. (As I write this, someone died in a crevasse on Mt. Rainier just last week). Usually we found a way around the cracks, but when that was not possible, you found the smallest gap you could and you jumped over it.

Four of the group members would lie down in the ice and grab what they can with their ice axe, and the fifth person would jump. If the jumper falls into the crack, the ropes should hold and the other four pull them out.

We had about seven jumps over crevasses we had to do. All went well, nobody fell in. But the jumping process takes a while.

We finally got to the top! It was tough to be too excited because there were indeed 75 mph winds. We had so much gear on and were roped up so we were not worried about getting blown away, but the winds were making us very cold. Very, very cold. Sure, we had cold weather gear on, but the winds were managing to cut through the gear to freeze us. So, we didn't want to stay long at the top.

Just for this climb Lorraine and I had bought a Nikon "Action Touch" camera—advertised as the best camera for hiking because it supposedly could get banged up and still work fine. I pulled the new camera out of my pack and pointed it at Lorraine. Nothing. It was frozen. I tried to warm it up. Nope. It would not work. Fortunately, Dan had a working camera, which he gave to the random guy we came up with who got a nice shot of the four of us who actually knew each other at the top with Dan's camera.

It was noon. We were alone at the top because many groups bailed, plus the standard is to summit by 9 am and head down while there is still some ice. As the snow gets warmed by the afternoon sun it gets slushier and more dangerous to climb down. The edges of those crevasses we had to jump, for example, could be mushy. We had spent so much time talking with groups that had decided to quit, that it put our group in extra jeopardy. Over 80% of the people who die climbing die on the way down, not up.

We spent only a couple of minutes at the top, in order to keep from freezing to death. We did not sign "the book." (My daughter Amanda signed it for us years later when she climbed Rainier). Once we got a few hundred feet down, the rocks around us kept the wind to a manageable level and we stopped freezing. We were still cold, but the extra effort it was taking because the snow was mushy actually helped keep us warm. Luckily we were all in good shape, or we would have been exhausted. Again, nobody fell into the seven crevasses we had to jump on the way down.

Dan did a great job as leader, and we got back down without incident. It was about 7 pm but still quite light out when we trudged into Camp Muir. Normally, folks spend the night there and hike out in the morning. Dan and his friend did that, but Lorraine and I chose to keep going back to the car. After all, after Muir it was just hiking, without need for crampons or ropes and there was enough light.

Turned out to be a bad plan. Following a snow trail is simple when there is only one trail. Turns out, when you get close to Paradise, there are lots of snow trails as many people come up to Paradise just to hike around. A snow trail can look different after one day from just more foot prints.

We took the wrong trail.

As someone once said, on a mountain all upward trails lead to the top, but only one downward trail leads to where you started.

By the time we realized we had taken a wrong turn, Lorraine started to complain that her knees were hurting. This was a sudden problem. She did not want to go back up the steep trail we came down to find the correct trail. Although we had camping gear, we were not in an area where we could easily set up a tent. We could find a spot, but I thought instead I was pretty sure where we had missed the correct trail. I left Lorraine with all the camping gear and food, etc. and went off (much lighter without my pack and gear) backtracking upward to find the correct downward trail. I did so, and found my way to Paradise—as I suspected we were not far off—where I spotted a couple of rangers. When I told them my story, they got all excited about the "injured climber" and we took a sled up to where Lorraine was, to "sled" her back to Paradise on the snow. By the time we got her onto the sled it was dark, but there were plenty of flashlights and the rangers knew a shortcut so rather than steep uphill then steep downhill as I had gone, it was a pretty level ride back to Paradise.

One of the rangers mentioned something about a helicopter evacuation, but Lorraine just wanted a ride to our car.

I agree with my brother-in-law about climbing Mount Rainier: "I wouldn't call it fun, but I am very glad I did it."

Top of Mt. Rainier. Dan's friend, Lorraine, Doug, Dan. Can you tell the winds were 75 mph?

Beach Fire with a Fireman—[Cousin Rick] We vacationed at

the beach with some friends, one of which is a fireman. When he found out that beach fires were legal, he went out Friday evening and built a big fire on the beach. The weather Friday night was misty and cold, so nobody wanted to go out to the beach that night.

So, he spent Saturday working on his fire. Saturday night was cool and dry. We went out.

The fire was huge. Taller than any of us.

Based on this experience, I am guessing that many firemen are actually fire fiends...?

Memorable Flight—We were touring an aircraft carrier in San

Diego when I asked a navy pilot about his most memorable flight. He said he was flying a supply plane with twin props off an aircraft carrier in the Mediterranean Sea and the weather was poor. He was supposed to go to a remote area of Turkey to get supplies. He landed in a big dirt field and loaded the supplies, but he looked around and didn't see any buildings. He wondered how he was going to refuel. Then he saw a pickup truck with a big open barrel of fuel approaching. They used a crazy mechanism to pour fuel into his plane from that open barrel without hoses. But, his plane was soon refueled, and he took off to go back. The weather was getting worse, and the waves were large enough to move the carrier around, making the landing tougher than usual. Then, he lost an engine. He could not restart it. No problem, he can land with one engine, but it is tougher, especially in bad weather. The instant he landed, his second engine quit and he could not restart it, either. The folks on the carrier were angry at him, because there were other planes that needed to land and it was a big hassle to winch the plane off the runway.

Later, the mechanics said both engines were not repairable and had to be scrapped. They both had leaves and twigs in the engine that had caused both engines to fail.

PHOTOGRAPHY

Almost Missed the Boat—Lorraine and I were wedding

photographers for a while. We enjoyed it. We got pretty good at it and it was fun to see all the different weddings. We did one wedding where it was a combination Jewish/Catholic wedding in a Catholic Church under a Chuppah. The bride and groom could not find a rabbi or a priest in Seattle willing to do the ceremony, but they found a willing priest in Arizona and flew him out. They had ten bridesmaids and ten groomsmen, and each couple did a different dance step as they made their way up the aisle.

The reception was on a large boat. There are many boats you can rent in Seattle for receptions, and the "Good Times" company had four boats. We were on the "Good Times III" boat, and as we pulled away from the dock, a couple came running "Oh my god I knew we were late but I didn't think we were this late!" yelled the woman and she jumped aboard while the boat pulled away. I watched her date behind her almost fall in, only to be caught by the deckhands and pulled on board.

Later, after we had taken the normal reception photos (cake, toast, etc.) we saw the most amazing sight—the sun was setting just as a school of whales were going by. I set up my camera and literally grabbed couples "Stand there, smile" I said, click, then grabbed another couple. I did about six couples and then I saw the couple who jumped on the boat late. They at first said no, but I insisted. I did about three more couples and the sun disappeared. I was glad to have gotten as many couples as I could in that perfect setting.

After the honeymoon, we showed all our photos to the bride and groom. The photo with the late couple, the sunset and whales came out particularly well, so it was prominently displayed. The bride and groom asked me, "Who are these people?"

Champaign for the Bride's Father—One wedding I tried to

take a photo of the bride and groom with the bride's father. There was a large bottle of Champaign in front of the father, so I tried to move it. What looked like one big long table, was actually several tables pushed together, and they were not quite at the same level. Where I put the bottle on the big tablecloth, turned out to be on the edge of two tables, such that the bottle tipped forward toward the father. I grabbed at it to pull it back, but it had slippery Champaign all over the bottle, and it slipped and fell forward. I grabbed two more times, each time and I pulled it back and the bottle slipped forward the Champaign spewed out higher and higher, spraying the father more and more. Rather than take a photo, it appeared that I was just spraying the father of the bride with Champaign.

Oops.

Romanian Wedding—We have only done one Romanian

wedding. We were told to arrive at 9 am, which we did, but the wedding had been going for 30 minutes at this point. The wedding lasted almost another four hours. It was all in Romanian, which I don't understand, but it appeared that everyone in the audience one by one went up to the microphone. Near the microphone there was a semi-circle of chairs where the groom, bride, groomsmen, bridesmaids and clergy were sitting, and behind that was a semi circle of 8-foot plastic columns with ferns at the top, then another semi-circle of chairs where a choir was sitting. After about 90 minutes the groom motioned to me (while—I swear—an audience member was playing an accordion). The groom started to whisper and I bent down to listen, but just then my camera bag over my shoulder shifted and hit one of those plastic columns. It fell and hit the next column like dominos, and suddenly all of the choir members had columns and ferns in their laps. Real ferns with real dirt, it turned out.

Everyone scrambled to get it all cleaned up, and the bride told me not to worry because it happens all the time (?).

For the next two hours, I stood near the front taking photos, and all eyes of the audience were on me, not the speakers. I have no idea what they were saying, but it seemed awfully warm in there.

Bar Mitzvahs—A professionally photographed Bar Mitzvah (or a Bat Mitzvah for that matter), tends to be at an expensive venue, which means that you have a gathering of formally dressed thirteen-year-olds. When you have a typical thirteen-year-old girl formally dressed, she looks 28. A thirteen-year-old boy formally dressed looks 8. Put them side-by-side for a photo and it looks like mom and son.

Photos as a Gift—At one wedding we photographed I noticed someone named Lenny beside me taking all the same photos I was taking. Lenny had the exact same camera I had. Lenny said that he was going to photograph the wedding as a gift and give the photos to the bride a groom. Hmmm, I thought. Here I was setting up all these photos and Lenny was taking the photos I set up from the same spot I was with the same camera, then giving them for free as a gift. I wondered if the bride and groom would resent paying us.

When we met with the bride and groom after they got back from their honeymoon to give them the photos we took, they told us how glad they were to get our photos because they were so much better than Lenny's. They were very disappointed with Lenny's photos.

Blue Tarp Wedding—We did a wedding under a giant blue tarp because it was an outdoor wedding beside a lake and the bride and groom did not trust the weather. Each guest had been given an inexpensive camera, and the bride and groom got all the photos from all their guests in addition to all of the photos we took.

When it was time to show the bride and groom our photos, the bride seemed nervous. When the bride saw our first photo of her alone she had a big sigh of relief, "My dress is white!" she exclaimed.

"Of course your dress is white." We were confused.

The bride had several thousand cheap camera photos from her guests of her wearing a blue dress.

Moms at Weddings—At every wedding, we get photographs of
the family members. One wedding was complicated, because the bride wanted pictures with her birth mother of course, then separate pictures with her dad and his third wife, and more pictures with her dad's second wife who was no relation to her, but was the woman the bride considered her "real" mother because this woman raised her from age two to age eighteen.

We spent so much time on the bride's family, I was a bit worried that we might run out of time for the groom's family. I need not have worried. His father did not attend and he didn't want any photos of his mom because of something his mom had said that morning.

New Wording—When you have photographed over a hundred
weddings like Lorraine and I did, you pretty much know what the minister is going to say. Which is why I almost dropped my camera when I was expecting the standard "so long as you both shall live" and instead heard "so long as this marriage shall last."

Married His Sister—I had a good friend who entered the clergy
and became a minister. When his sister and her fiancé decided to get

married, Lorraine and I photographed the wedding, and my friend performed the ceremony. Thus, I watched my friend marry his sister.

Largest audience for a wedding we ever saw.

FAMILY

Gram—My mother's mother was the ultimate optimist. We used to say that in an earthquake she would be remarking about how nice the new buildings would be. I didn't see too much of her, but I do have a couple of memories of her when we visited when I was about ten years old.

She had bad knees. She had trouble especially getting out of cars. She would talk the entire time, "Let's try my right knee today. Nope. I guess not today. Ok, let's try my left knee then. Oh, I don't think so. Maybe my right knee has reconsidered. Nope. Maybe my left wants to make it up to me. No. Maybe we can try them both together. There! That worked! Good thing I am not a centipede!"

She liked to give her many grandkids of differing ages a small change purse with a nickel and two pennies in each one. This was in the 1960s when penny candy existed, but still seven cents was not much. Of course, she did it to make sure everyone got exactly the same thing, so there would be no complaints. After she gave out the change purses, my 21-year-old cousin Billy came storming in a pretend huff. "I heard all the OTHER grandkids got a SHINY penny, except me!" He cried, pointing to the two dull pennies in his purse. Gram pretended to be horrified. "I'll shine one myself!" she cried.

Family Reunion—At a family reunion one year, everyone wore a hat that said "Rough Family Reunion" and someone walked by and said "Boy I've been THERE!"

Farming Fertilizer—My cousin at a family reunion told the story of his farming neighbor after a severe storm knocked out electricity including water pumps. This meant they had no water, including no water to flush their toilets. No problem. His neighbor's wife went into their field after the storm passed to do her business, and a news chopper came by and hovered over her field to survey the storm damage. She tried to wave them away, but they just waved back. Footage of her was on the local news, but fortunately you could not tell what she was doing besides waving.

Who IS That?—I was walking down the street one day in Seattle, and I could see someone coming toward me on the sidewalk that looked familiar, but I could not place him. I did not know if I should stop him. I decided not to stop him as I could not remember why I knew him. We passed each other.

About two minutes later, I remembered: "Oh, yeah, he is my brother!"

My step-brother, whom I had met once at my father's wedding three years previously.

My Tour of Dad's Office—I decided at the age of 27 that I was going to visit my dad at Boeing. He had never invited me or any of my siblings to where he worked, but I invited myself. After going, I got a sense of why no one had been invited.

I was not allowed to photograph anything. The first building, "Plant 2" I believe it was called, was a sea of I estimate about three hundred desks, all facing the same direction, about fifteen desks side-to-side with about twenty rows. Each desk had two cords hanging down from the ceiling, one that looked like a phone cord and one that looked like a power cord. The word "sweatshop" came to mind. My father's desk was not in this array. No cubicles of any kind.

Over on one side was a bank of elevators. His desk was there, so that those waiting for the elevators or getting off the elevators were at his back. His was the only desk situated this way, facing a wall. Certainly preferable to the sea of desks with draped cords, but not exactly ideal.

As he worked mainly in the military area, there was tape on the floor and signs overhead marking the area beyond which anyone without military clearance could not go. Several people were careful to make sure I stayed on the correct side of the tape as I had no military clearance.

I am no expert, but one or more walls might have been useful....

My Dad Dies—In many ways, after my mother died, my father tried to commit slow suicide. He began drinking about a half gallon of whisky per week when my mom got cancer when I was in high school. He worked up to about twice that. Boeing was pretty tolerant for many years until he retired. He must have done a good job there. He always smoked, but he started smoking more, up to five packs per day. He would leave a lit one somewhere and light up a new one when he left the room rather than go back for the lit one, so not all those cigs got fully smoked.

And he argued. One of his favorite things to argue about was how the studies linking smoking and cancer were wrong. Two years before he died, he got throat cancer, which studies link to the combination of smoking and drinking. To his credit, after his throat cancer operation, he quit smoking cold turkey. Not drinking, though. Not by a long shot.

After a while, the throat cancer returned and migrated to his lungs. He had to have surgery on his lungs, but some folks were optimistic. I remember talking to a father of one of the girls on Carolyn's soccer team. He was a surgeon, and said he was very familiar with my dad's procedure. He said it was no big deal, normally, and he should recover quickly. He then asked me if my father drank much. I told him my father was a severe alcoholic. His eyes got big. He didn't say anything more, but he didn't need to. His eyes told me my father would not survive the lung surgery operation. His eyes were right.

After the surgery, my father got pneumonia, which is typical after lung surgery. However, antibiotics which normally cure it do not work if the blood is full of alcohol. Doctors said my father was on an alcohol drip, because his alcoholism was so bad that if his alcohol intake was stopped, his heart would stop. So, he would either die from his heart stopping from no alcohol, or from the pneumonia. We chose the pneumonia. In the end, it was me the doctors asked when it was time to turn off the machine keeping him alive. The numbers were falling, it was clear the machines would only keep him alive at most another couple of hours. My brother and sisters did not want to make the call or were not asked. I said okay. He died in December 1994.

He was a tough man to like. I salute my mom and his second wife, Sue, who both loved him dearly.

He was buried alongside my mom in a plot with a double headstone ready for him—purchased and placed back in 1973 when my mom died.

Two months after my father died my brother was in a meeting near the cemetery. He didn't often get to that area as he lives in Port Townsend. After the meeting, my brother told the other folks at the meeting to go on ahead because he wanted to visit the cemetery. Someone said, "Yes, I am sorry, I remember your father died recently."

And my brother said, "Oh, yeah, you are right."

My brother wanted to visit mom.

I am with by brother. If I go to the cemetery, I go to visit mom.

I guess if I looked at things differently I could thank dad for not signing papers for Whitman College so I ended up going to Western Washington and meeting Lorraine, and for not helping me financially in college so I would be forced to figure out how to pay for it all, and for getting me to hate cigarettes and alcohol and arguments which makes me healthier, and for making me deeply want to be a better father than, well, you-know-who. But I am not able to thank him for all that right now.

Maybe later.

Afghan Learning—Warning: the following story is as I understand
it. Every time I try and get the story straight from my cousin Toc she says I
have some details wrong. But it is still an interesting story. Toc's real
name is Carolyn. She is the first child of Tom and Carolyn, who wrote
letters to their family calling their future first child TOC meaning Tom (if a
son), or Carolyn (if a daughter), but she has been called Toc all her life.

In the mid-1960s, my cousin Toc was in the Peace Corps in Afghanistan.
She became friends with a girl named Sakena, who wanted to become a
doctor. In the 1960s girls did not become doctors in Afghanistan. So,
basically Tom and Carolyn sponsored Sakena to come to Dearborn,
Michigan where they lived, to become a doctor with the full intention of
Sakena going back some day to Afghanistan.

Toc became a corporate lawyer for Ford Motor Company. Sakena became
a doctor.

War broke out in Afghanistan in the 1970s, and educated people were at
risk of being thrown in jail or killed. Sakena sponsored her family to come
to Dearborn because she was worried they would otherwise be killed.
Sakena's family then sponsored more families.

To this day, there are more Afghans in Dearborn, Michigan per capita than
any other city in the US.

Toc and Sakena wanted to help the Afghan people. Sakena formed the
Afghan Institute of Learning (AIL). Toc formed Creating Hope International
(CHI). Two connected charities. AIL set up underground schools for girls in
Afghanistan. This was under the Taliban, and it had to be secret because
girls were not supposed to go to school under the Taliban. They also set
up clinics for women because women were not allowed to disrobe in
Taliban clinics. It is difficult to treat many diseases when you cannot see
the skin.

Because AIL was supposed to be secret, CHI was set up to try and provide funding. I may have some of this wrong. But imagine the difficulty of raising funds for a secret activity that is illegal in the affected country.

Anyhow, at the time of the US invasion of Afghanistan, there were between 70 and 80 underground schools and 7 women's clinics being run by AIL.

If you like TED talks (www.TED.com), search for "Sakena" and you can hear her tell the following story, which I will shorten up a bit here.

Sakena had an office in Afghanistan to run AIL, because it was a huge undertaking. Girls were not allowed to travel anywhere alone, so every girl had to have a male escort to and from each underground school. Meanwhile, if 50 girls all showed up at some house at once, it would be obvious that it was a school, so each arrival and departure had to be timed to not cause suspicion. Not to mention, books, lessons, computers, etc. Somebody had to keep track.

Sakena had an office with several other people. Some of the folks in her office were traveling one day in a vehicle and were stopped by 19 Taliban soldiers. The leader pointed to Sakena and told her to get out. They all had guns. Her bodyguard tried to intervene. The Taliban insisted that Sakena get out of the car.

Sakena got out. When it was clear the Taliban did not want the other office folks, they fled. Sakena never saw them again. The 19 soldiers marched Sakena down an alley to a secluded spot.

The leader said "We know what you are doing, don't deny it. We know you are teaching girls about computers and business skills." Sakena decided it was no use denying it. She admitted what he said was true.

She was fairly certain she was going to die any minute, unless she got "lucky" and was sent to prison. Remember that she is a US-trained doctor who could have chosen to be in Michigan playing golf.

The leader looked at her sternly and said, "What about us boys?"

The Taliban schools did not teach boys these topics. He wanted schools for boys to learn about computers and business skills, just like the girls.

Sakena and AIL ended up forming underground schools for boys, too. Many of those soldiers ended up helping the schools. But she had to hire new staff to replace those that fled.

Toc told me once that she can no longer go to Afghanistan as there are many people who would shoot her on sight. Both Toc and Sakena put their own lives at risk for the Afghan people. They are true heroes.

Clary—The strangest story of my life. My wife's mother had a long-term boyfriend she called "Clary." Clary worked as a tugboat operator for Crowley Marine. Sometimes tugboat operations kept Clary away for days or even months, but he was usually around for holidays and such unless he was with his daughter from a previous marriage. I would go with Lorraine to visit her mom maybe six or seven times per year and Clary was there about half the time. Clary was a nice, quiet fellow. He and I did not have a lot in common as I don't fish or even own a boat. (I sometimes tell people I own a boat but haven't blown it up in a while). He mostly kept to himself.

One day I was riding the bus to work and I started talking to a guy sitting next to me. His name was Kirk, and he was about my age. Kirk told me he was an accountant for Crowley Marine in their main headquarters. I asked him how often he got on a tug boat and he said "never." I started to ask Kirk if he knew Clary, then realized I didn't know Clary's last name, and the way my wife's mom called him "Clary" it sounded like a pet name, plus I thought an accountant might only see real, given names rather than nicknames. So I asked Kirk if he knew anyone out on the boats named "Clarence something-or-other." I admitted I didn't know the guy's last name. Kirk said no, the name was not familiar to him. Clary was a good

25 years older than this guy, who looked to be in his late 30s, so this did not surprise me. I asked for his business card and made a mental note to show Kirk's card to Clary when I next saw him, in case Clary knew the guy or even knew what Crowley Marine business cards looked like.

I forgot about Kirk's card in my wallet for about two years. Meanwhile, Kirk stopped riding my bus and I never saw Kirk again. But one day we were at Lorraine's mom's house and Clary said something about numbers supplied by accountants at Crowley Marine headquarters and I remembered the card in my wallet. Clary happened to be eating a snack from a plate (it was not meal-time), so I set the card next to his plate and asked him if he knew the guy. I was surprised at myself for remembering after a couple of years. Clary mumbled something about not knowing the guy, which did not particularly surprise me, and Clary changed the subject. Oh, well. I took the card back and looked for somewhere to throw it away, glad that now I had a slightly thinner wallet.

Fast forward about fifteen years, during which we did not see much of Clary, due to his trips, staying with his daughter and his various illnesses. Lorraine told me one day that Clary was in a hospice and not expected to live more than a week. The next day, I got my first-ever and only phone call from Clary. He was short: "Doug, I'd like to see you" was all he said and hung up. I hadn't spoken much to him in 15 years, and now this. During the 35-minute drive to the hospice, I could not for the life of me figure out why he wanted to see me.

When I got to the hospice, I asked a doctor where Clary was and was directed to his room. "How much did he pay you?" Clary demanded when I walked in. I said, "What?" (The doctor I just spoke to? I wondered. Why would he pay me?). Clary persisted, "How much did Kirk pay you?" I didn't remember who Kirk was at this point. "Kirk who?" I asked. "Kirk's card! How much did he pay you to slap that business card in my face?" At this point, I pieced it together. "You knew him after all? He said he didn't recognize your name."

When we sorted it all out, it turns out that Kirk had been the one who broke up Clary's first marriage! Clary said Kirk was a real jerk (but a pleasant enough fellow on the bus in my experience). Clary's real name was Clary, and had I asked Kirk about that name, he might have known who I was talking about. I finally convinced Clary that I didn't know anything about what Kirk had done or not done, Kirk did not know I had shown Clary the card, plus I hadn't seen Kirk in 15 years or more. Clary then admitted that he had purposely not spoken to me for 15 years (and I had not noticed because Clary was not someone I went out of my way to converse with).

In the end, Clary forgave me on his death bed for the insult I had unintentionally given him 15 years previously. May he rest in peace.

$100 Bowl—In the 1960s, my mom made a bowl, which she called her "$100 Bowl." That used to be a lot of money. When she added up the cost of the class she took, the materials (it took her many tries), plus the bowl she bought as a mold, the cost of that bowl was $100. So she said.

I have it now. Frankly, as bowls go it is amateurish, flimsy and tips easily.

It is my most prized possession.

NEW YORK LIFE

Hired by New York Life—After 30 years of writing computer
models to do financial planning, strategic planning and forecasting, I
retired from SCL. The retirement system at SCL is set up so that you
maximize your benefits after 30 years. It did not make sense to stay
beyond 30 years.

I was only 52 years old, and wanted to keep working. The easy thing to do
would have been to go to another electric utility and keep doing what I
was doing. However, one thing I noticed was that most people do not
properly plan. I wanted a job where I could help people plan properly.

I was at my dentist, Sydney, the one who used to be on the Chargers girls
soccer team I coached in high school, and mentioned to her (as she had
various things in my mouth) that I was looking for a job where I could help
people plan properly. She said her husband worked for New York Life
(NYL) and was hiring.

Sydney Walters has my vote for best dentist, by the way, not that I have
tried them all.

I spent seven years at NYL. Compared to SCL, NYL had better
management, in my opinion. SCL's management problems stem from
being a utility where the leader is not a politician but reports to a
politician (the mayor of Seattle). The mayor is not elected based on his
knowledge of electricity.

A lot of management at SCL was trying to assign blame. Cover your butt,
was what everyone was taught to do. I remember after a month at NYL I
made a rookie mistake. My boss asked me to come into his office and
close the door behind me. Oh, boy. At SCL, that meant bad things.
Yelling, sometimes. At NYL, my boss leaned toward me and said, "How
can I help?" I thought I misheard him. I wondered why he was not
screaming.

What People Really Want—I was naïve when I started at NYL. I thought since I was an expert—I have over 30 years of computer modeling experience, plus an MBA, plus various licenses (Series 6, 7, 63, life, etc.). I thought people wanted advice from an expert. Silly me. They don't. People actually want to be sold. They do. They just think they don't want to be sold. They are mixed up. They think they are being "sold" when someone gives an expert opinion. They are more likely to act when told to do so by someone who has good sales skills but is not an expert, than they are by someone is an expert who does not have the sales skills. I know, I am the guy who is the expert without sales skills watching non-experts with good sales skills.

I am pretty open about what I do. I tell people: Based on my thorough expert analysis you should do such-and-such. Yes, I sell those products. Yes, I get a commission if you buy them.

Good-bye, say most people. Don't come back.

I understand that everyone needs to have an automatic "no" response to pretty much everything new these days because there are so many frauds. But getting to "yes" should be based on trust and expertise, not sales skills. Not the "expertise" of "I just attended this seminar" or "I just read this book" but years of training or college.

You should want a win-win situation in all dealings. Both parties of a transaction should be happy.

Here is what most people don't get: You should have someone you trust help you with your money, not someone good at sales. Someone you have known for years, preferably, or someone people you trust have known for years. More than ten years of being trustworthy should be your deciding factor.

They don't have to be middle-aged. You may personally know a 25-year-old with 15 years of trustworthy behavior.

Someone told me he never wants a friend to help him with money. I understand that he doesn't want to lose a friend if something goes wrong. But here is what that person does not understand—you have to trust someone, and the choice between trusting a stranger and trusting a friend should be easy. And if they are a long-time friend, they will be motivated to keep your friendship, which is an added incentive for them to do a good job.

Taking financial advice from someone who is not a well-trained good friend or a well-trained good friend of a friend is dumb, in my opinion.

And guess what? The talking heads on TV and the internet are NOT your friends.

First Book—Because a proper financial analysis is based on the future, and nobody knows the future, the best path forward is careful diversification including at least some safe money. Many people don't get that, so I decided to write a book on proper financial planning. The title of the book is "Do You Have ANY Save Money?" because everyone, and especially every business, should have some safe money, defined as guaranteed and likely to beat inflation. I also throw in legal protections, tax benefits and theft protections in what I call safe money. It is the starting point, I believe, for a good financial framework. Safe money is what I have found most people and businesses lack in their financial planning.

It took me about six months to write the book. I got advice and editing help from many folks, including my MBA professors.

I found out a few interesting things in writing this book. First, if you have training and licenses like I do, then the government can regulate what you say in your book if you are talking about financial planning. The regulations are so severe, that nearly all people with training and licenses do not publish books on financial planning. The regulations do not apply to those who have no licenses or training.

Think about what that means for a second—virtually all books published on financial planning are by authors who do not have training or licenses. In other words, virtually every book on financial planning (except mine, of course) is junk!

One sample regulation: I can give away or sell the book you are reading to whomever I please because it is not on financial advice, but I must only sell my book on financial advice. I cannot give it away.

NYL told me flat out that I could not continue as an employee if I published the financial advice book due to these regulations. Unfortunately, they did not tell me this until after I had written it. I decided to quit NYL—no hard feelings—and publish the book anyway in 2016. I self-published through Amazon.

From the few books from other authors on the subject I read, I can tell you that to the extent they do any analysis at all, they often do it incorrectly. It is frustrating for me as an analyst, because I have read some of the most popular authors, and they have some great advice on saving, making a budget, etc. then tell people to not do something that my analysis says makes sense to do, or to do something that my analysis says is foolish. They provide no analysis for what they are saying, so it is my analysis against no analysis.

I am not yet certain I will be able to keep my licenses since I published this book. A final determination has not been made yet. It is a risk I am willing to take.

Anyway, take a look at my introduction for free at www.doyouhaveanysafemoney.com

And sorry, I cannot give it away.

SOCCER

Finding Mickey—I had a very good friend named Mickey on my soccer team in the third grade. Mickey and I lived about two blocks away from each other, but walking between our houses did not involve any busy streets, so our parents let us third graders walk back and forth between our houses often. At the end of third grade Mickey moved away and I was quite sad. I heard that he moved about ten miles away, but I didn't know where.

After I graduated from college, I was playing on a men's soccer team, and I was defending a forward whose teammates called him "Mickey." I had only known one "Mickey" in my life and that was my buddy in third grade. The guy I was guarding did not look at all like my third grade buddy. Then he laughed. I knew that laugh! It was him! The next time the ball went out of bounds, I introduced myself to him, as he, too, did not recognize me. Puberty can make big changes between third grade and college. The next time he got the ball, he obviously decided that he was going to dribble around me, and I, of course, decided there was no way he was going to get by me. We went back and forth the full width of the field, and then hit a hole in the poorly maintained field and we both tripped. Our legs tangled and the ball rolled away. We laughed and laughed, while our teammates didn't get the joke.

I tried to get together with Mickey and our wives, but it was nearly impossible, due to Mickey's wife. I suggested that the four of us go to a sporting event or a movie or a play. She said she didn't like any of those. I suggested hiking, biking, golf or skiing. She didn't like outdoor things. Board games or cards? She didn't like those either. I asked her what she liked to do. She said she liked to crochet. I asked her what she liked to do that others could do as well. She said she liked to watch soap operas on TV. At that point I decided that an activity without her was the only option.

Mickey and I got together a couple of times after that, going fishing, boating and then I kind of "lost" him again for a couple of years.

When I worked in downtown Seattle, I always went for a walk at lunchtime. One day a couple of years later I came up behind someone obviously depressed. I could tell from the back this person was as sad as anyone I had ever seen. It turned out to be Mickey. He had just filed for divorce. He said he tried so hard to make it work. I didn't know what to say. I was not his wife's biggest fan, but I thought it best to just say I was sorry for him. He didn't want to talk.

A couple of years later, again walking at lunch I came upon someone who looked as happy and joyful as anyone I had ever seen. You guessed it— Mickey. He had met someone, and was in love. He seemed to be walking a few inches off the ground.

My wife and I were invited to Mickey's second wedding, and the two of them seemed like a much better match to me. They moved quite a distance away, so I lost Mickey again, but I suspect he is much happier these days.

On my lunchtime walks I only saw Mickey twice, and he was both the saddest and happiest person I ever saw.

Gil—[Cousin Rick] Wally was the manager of a men's soccer team I played on and Gil was one of my teammates. Wally had an interesting way of talking such that no matter what he said, he sounded like he was apologizing. Gil thought it was hilarious to get Wally mad at him because Wally seemed to apologize to Gil when Gil did something wrong.

I met Gil for lunch one day at his office at a bank and Gil introduced me to his boss. Are you a computer programmer? Gil's boss asked me. I admitted I was. Here is what I want you to do, he said. He spent about five minutes describing a task he needed to be automated. How much are you going to charge me? He asked. I said, I hadn't given it much thought.

I ended up writing a "flooring" program that kept track of the amount of money car dealerships owed the bank when they borrowed money to buy cars to then sell. That program ended up saving the bank the equivalent of three full-time employees. I only charged him $1200.

I should have given it more thought.

Gil ended up getting his boss' daughter pregnant and last I heard he moved to Florida. When you want to get away from the state of Washington, Florida is a popular choice.

Shin Guards—As a long-time soccer player, I originally thought shin guards were dumb. Referees required that you wear them, so I kept two copies of Readers Digest in my car as emergency shin guard in case I forgot my real shin guards. Referees didn't care what shin guards were made of, but would not let you play without them.

In High School, after I had played for many years, my PE class had a soccer unit. Easy for those of us who had played many years.

I was happy that the PE class did nor require shin guards. This made my footwork slightly faster. I came up against someone who played football, but had never played soccer. With quick footwork, I easily took the ball around him, but he swung his foot at the ball (and missed, of course) so hard that he hit my shin and broke my leg. Shin guards would have helped.

The next session in PE was dance, and I couldn't do it because I had a broken leg.

Lack of shin guards made me a lousy dancer.

Canadian Soccer—While I was at WWU I played in a Canadian soccer league. Thus, every away game was in Canada, and so the team crossed the border many times. Four incidents were memorable:

1. A guy named Davood from Iran played on our team, but only when we had a home game. Someone asked him why. He said due to his immigration status, it would be difficult but not impossible to cross the border. One game we talked him into going to Canada. When the guard asked the full van if everyone was a US Citizen, only Davood said no. The van was pulled aside and we were called into a room, where Davood got out a suitcase full of papers and started to pull them out. The border guard was surrounded by 17 soccer players with crossed arms asking how long this was going to take. After glancing at the first few papers and the crowd around him, he gave the papers back to Davood and said he was going to grant him honorary US Citizenship just for the day.

2. The team crossed the border at Sumas. Sumas is a town on the US border, but there is nothing on the Canadian side there. We wanted to wait for another vehicle after crossing the border, so we parked on the Canadian side after crossing. While waiting, I decided to go to the store about a hundred feet from where we were parked. An overweight guard came huffing and puffing out of the booth. "What are you doing?" Oops. I guess I was accidently re-crossing the border.

3. I was hired to referee a soccer game in Canada. When crossing the border, I made the mistake of telling the guard that. He took me into an office and asked if I was getting paid. I hope so, I said. Then I needed a work permit, and that usually takes weeks. OK, I said, but you are going to have 22 disappointed Canadians if you turn me back and good luck getting a Canadian to referee today. He let me through.

4. It was a home game in Bellingham against a Canadian team we had played before. At one point a player on each team tried to kick the ball when it was chest high, their legs hit and there was a

loud CRACK! Almost before the injured player from my team hit the ground, someone had dialed 911. The fire station it turned out was less than a block away although you could not see it from the field. The aid unit seemed to arrive in seconds. They pulled up with a stretcher, asked a couple of quick questions, used some device to immobilize the leg, used a scooping device to put him on the stretcher, and he was off the field in the aid car in less than a minute. The Canadian I was guarding said, "Wow! If I ever break my leg, I want to break it RIGHT HERE!"

Worst Referee Ever—When I was in my late 20s I was playing on a men's soccer team (not the Shamrocks), and there was controversy over what happened in a particular play.

Everyone agrees on this part: The ball was crossed (kicked) head high into my team's goal mouth. I was defending a forward from the other team and we were about two feet apart. There was no pushing. We both jumped up to head the ball, there was a collision in the area of our heads, the ball went off the forward's head then mine, and we both fell down in pain. I began bleeding from a major wound in my forehead.

What the referee claimed happened: I banged the forward with my head striking his head causing my head to bleed. I committed violent conduct so I was shown a red card and the other team was awarded a penalty kick.

Red cards are a big deal in recreational leagues. If a player gets one, that player is fined, and cannot play in the next game. If a player then gets a second, that player is typically banned from the league for life.

What everyone else, including players on both teams claimed happened: The forward swung his elbow around in an attempt to gain power for his planned heading of the ball. His elbow hit my forehead and caused a major injury. As I was bleeding on the ground in pain, I asked the forward why he was writhing in pain as well. He told me and his teammates that he thought he broke his elbow.

Any other referee in the world would have given the forward a red card for violent conduct for swinging an elbow at my face.

I was in the hospital getting 27 stitches in my forehead, but I am told my team protested the penalty by refusing to put a goalie into the goal for the penalty kick. The other team felt badly about the lousy call, but not so badly that they missed the kick on an empty net.

My team protested my red card to the league. The league said they would not rescind my red card without a signed statement from the forward involved.

Right. Hey elbow guy, if you sign this statement, you'll get a fine, you will not be able to play in the next game, and you'll be half way to being banned in soccer for life. How about it?

Shamrocks—I joined many soccer teams in the Seattle area. At one point I was playing on three teams at once. I played on indoor and outdoor, men's and coed teams. I was good, but not great. I enjoyed playing any position, but usually midfield. When you play on as many teams as I did fall-winter-spring and summer, many teams fold so you join others, you end up knowing a lot of people by their first name only.

And sometimes there are people you didn't know you know, like the time I went to 60 acres park, which has almost 30 soccer fields, and I forgot which soccer field I was supposed to play on. Someone playing on field 5 called out "Hey Doug, you are on field 16!"—I still don't know who that was or why he knew, but he was right.

One of the few teams in all those 40+ years of playing soccer that did not eventually fold was the Shamrocks. The Shamrocks grew. From one team to four, playing in different age brackets. The "original" Shamrocks—

which I am not quite one because I have only been with the team since 1984 and it started in 1977—play in the "Over 55" league and next year in the "Over 60" league. Then there is a team in the "Over 50" league and one in the "Over 40" league and even a team in the "Over 30" league.

One year the Shamrocks decided to form a charity. They call it "Shamrock Charities" all for children (www.shamrockcharities.org). Originally just an excuse to get all of the guys in all the soccer teams together to play a charity golf tournament, it has grown. Imagine an entire golf course filled with people who would much rather kick the ball than hit it with a stick. Several players on the Seattle Sounders professional soccer team have played in the tournament or been a spokesperson for it.

What makes a team fold? Usually a single butthead can ruin a team, so everyone wants to quit. The Shamrocks have no buttheads!

Shamrock Golf—The Shamrock Charities golf tournament

(shamrockcharities.org), put on by the Shamrock men's soccer team(s) is a hoot. Most of the players play golf just once per year at this tournament, and it shows. The golf is not taken very seriously. Half-way through the tournament once the "spotters" for the hole where you get a prize if you get a hole-in-one told me that no one had yet landed on the green in one shot, much less gotten a hole-in-one. For one hole you have to use your driver for all hits, including putting. One hole is the "Happy Gilmore" hole where you have to run while you hit your drive. You get the idea. A player named Steve from the original team died, and so everyone on the 11th hole is supposed to take a shot of whisky in honor of Steve. One hole where you can only see the top of the flag the foursome ahead of you will often move the flag into the sand trap. At the tournament, I find balls that have "This ain't your damn ball" written on them where I thought my ball was.

Great fun.

Counting Beers—I have played soccer most of my life. As an adult, I usually played year-round. Normally the team would go to a tavern after each game.

Jim always knows the closest tavern to any given soccer field because they are "customers" of his "business." So he says. After the game, we would always follow Jim.

I cannot count the number of taverns I have been in, most of them multiple times. Even so, I can count the total number of beers I have consumed in my entire life. For most people, counting all beers would involve estimating. For me, I know the exact number.

Zero. I hate beer. I have spat it out the few times I have tried it.

Vegas Quarters—The Shamrocks men's soccer team that I played on for many years started going to a soccer tournament in Las Vegas every year in January. We would stay as a team in one of the hotel/casinos on "The Strip" and find our way to the soccer fields for games. I remember one time in the lobby waiting for ride while wearing our uniforms just before a game when Dave pulled out some quarters from his pocket and said, "I don't want these jangling in my pocket the whole game" and put them in a slot machine and pushed the button (no handles to pull these days). Ding, ding, ding. Dave won big. Quarters started pouring out. The machine ran out of quarters! Dave asked if they could write him a check. No. They had to refill the machine so it could continue pouring out quarters. He eventually won 1000 quarters ($250) and we were late for the game.

Moment of Silence—We drew the worst game at the Las Vegas soccer tournament one year, the first game. It started at 8 am. Nobody is ready for rigorous activity on a Saturday at 8 am in Las Vegas. We all sleepily stumbled to the game, more or less on time. Shannon, our goalie, was drunk and had not slept all night. So, we started to arrange for our backup goalie to play but Shannon got upset, insisting that he was "fine" and could do it. We tested him with a few shots and he did okay, and nobody wanted to argue with him, so he went out with everyone into positions to start.

The founder of this tournament years ago had just died, so the referee called for a moment of silence before blowing the whistle to start the game. We all bowed our heads and then Shannon screamed at the top of his lungs, "Go Shamrocks! Moment of Silence!" John, an attorney on the team, turned to me and whispered "Who screams 'moment of silence!' during a moment of silence?" I whispered, "Shannon, that's who!"

We won 2-1, and Shannon actually made a nice save.

Retired by a Fart—I was talking to one of the guys on the over-55 Shamrocks soccer team who told me he had retired. I was a little surprised as he had worked at the same company for many years and it seemed a bit early. He told me that his boss of many years called a meeting one day. He knew his boss hated public speaking, even though this was a relatively small group of managers at his company. They were in one of those rooms where they have folding wooden curtains that can make the room much bigger if the curtains are opened, but they were closed. He felt a fart coming on while his boss was speaking, and knew his boss would be upset if anyone heard it because everyone would laugh and his boss would think they were laughing at him, so he backed his way to the wall to be farther away. He backed into the wooden curtain. It turns out that a wooden curtain in a V-shape actually acts as an amplifier.

As predicted, his boss was not pleased by the laughter, and he knew the other managers would never let him forget it. He chose to retire rather than continue to work with mangers kidding him about his amplified fart.

Sounders Season Ticketholders—The Seattle Sounders

professional soccer team started in 1974. As I mentioned, I was at the first game. The team played for a while, then the league disbanded. Another team was formed and called itself the Seattle Sounders, even though that team played at a lower level, like AAA baseball compared to the majors. When a top-level professional soccer league in the US was again formed, Seattle wanted a franchise. They asked the season ticket holders to choose the name for this new team from three choices, none of which was "Seattle Sounders." Even so, the name "Seattle Sounders" won based on write-in votes.

One of the smart things that the Sounders did was let folks be season ticket holders without assigning them seats, so that you had a couple of months to try and find people you knew who also had season tickets to sit with. As a result, I have season tickets to the Seattle Sounders and sit with a bunch of folks on the Shamrocks soccer team I have played on since 1984 (with a few playing gaps due to my heart surgeries).

One of the dumb things the Sounders did was require people who brought banners to arrive 30 minutes early. Or was that a smart thing?

Consistently Good Choices—Ray, one of the Shamrock soccer

team guys, has a party every year at his house. His invitations say that you can bring your dog if the dog makes "consistently good choices." Recently at one of Ray's parties I kidded Ray by telling him that I did not make consistently good choices. Without missing a beat, Ray said, "Then you'll have to stay out on the lawn."

Newbies—When a fifteen-year-old joins any sports team these days,

they should expect that other players are likely to have ten or so years of experience. That is certainly true of girls soccer. When I was coaching my daughter Tessa's team one year we got two newbies. These were girls that had never played any sports before, and were starting in soccer against a bunch of girls with ten years of playing experience. As a coach of a recreational team I have to play these girls, and I needed to get them ready in a hurry.

In one of the first practices, we did what I call the Screamer drill. This is where the newbie stands about two feet in front of the back goal post and other players kick the ball low as hard as they can from the corner straight at them parallel to the goal line. A low screamer. The newbie is supposed to redirect the ball into the goal. Simple for someone who has a few years of experience. Tough for a newbie. It helps keep them from being afraid of a strong kick. We spent about 20 minutes on this Screamer drill.

Two weeks later, our best player was triple-teamed in a game. The other team forced her into the corner. She had few options. She managed to send a low Screamer across the mouth of the goal. One of our newbies was two feet in front of the back post, unguarded (because who guards a newbie?) and she redirected the ball into the goal.

We won the game on a goal by a newbie that was an exact copy of a drill we had recently spent 20 minutes on.

That never happens.

Fewer Than 11 on the Ferry—When I worked at Seattle City
Light, at one point I sat next to a guy named Mike, who lived on Bainbridge Island and played soccer for the Bainbridge Island men's team, which played in a Seattle league. He told me that on game day the team would get on the ferry to cross Puget Sound to Seattle and count noses. If there were not enough players, they could not call someone on the Island, since by the time the person called caught the next ferry, they would miss the game. As a result, they had a list of players on the "Seattle side" to call

if they needed more players. I got on that list, and about once or twice a year for fifteen years, I played soccer with the Bainbridge Island team. Then, someone asked me if I would just like to be on the team. I said okay. Playing on two teams was not forbidden, and if they played against the Shamrocks I was a traitor and played on the Shamrocks side.

So, having never lived on Bainbridge Island, and having hardly ever even gone there, I ended up playing for the Bainbridge island men's soccer team, even if there were 11 or more on the ferry. Unless I was a traitor that day.

Soccer Bloopers—I don't have videos of these, but I'll try to describe them as best I can.

1) I was playing forward, and I was running full tilt at the other team's goal. A guy on my team sent a low screamer (see *Newbies*) across the goal mouth. I stuck my leg out and hit the ball as I slid into the goal and I got tangled in the back net. The ball went straight up, rolled over the crossbar, then rolled down the back netting, hitting me in the head.

2) I played in high school with Terry Hickey, who later played for the Seattle Sounders. In one game Terry had the ball at his feet facing his own goal about two feet away, and opposing players on each shoulder. Not a good place to be. Trying to keep the other team from scoring from two feet away is tough when you are double-teamed. Most people would try to turn one way or the other and hope for the best. Not Terry. He flipped the ball up somehow and it landed on his head and stayed there. He then turned around keeping the ball still. He dropped the ball from his head to his foot and kicked it away before it hit the ground. I still remember the shocked, open mouth expressions of the two players on the other team.

3) I was playing on a team where we were getting beaten badly. Teams I played on didn't do as well as teams I coached. We were

playing with a goal net that had a hole, about twice the size of a soccer ball on the left side. The other team sent a ball to the back side of our left goal post that went through that hole and into the main net. The referee said it scored, when it actually didn't. I didn't protest too much as we were already behind 4-0. Ten minutes later, the other team kicked a ball that did score, but went through that hole the other way missing all netting, and the referee did not count it. The final score was 7-0 and correct, but the referee got two goals wrong.

4) We had an indirect free kick about 12 yards from the other team's goal. That meant that everyone had to stand at least 10 yards away. In this case, pretty much everyone stood within two yards of the goal. Indirect meant that you could not score a goal unless someone touched the ball besides the kicker. One of the guys on the team I played with was about 6 foot 8 and quite a clown—he danced around in front of the other team's goalkeeper, jumping and waving his arms. Just as the kicker from our team kicked the ball, he dropped flat to the ground. The ball hit the opposing goalkeeper in the face, and went in. Because somebody touched it, in this case the goalkeeper with his face, it counted as a goal.

5) My favorite soccer blooper. The other team sent a low screamer across the goal mouth from the right side. A forward from the other team about three feet in front of our goal took a big swing at the ball with his right leg and missed. The ball hit his left leg and stopped about two inches in the air, "trapped" by his left leg. Nothing but our net in front of him. He pulled his right leg back to try again, and accidently back-heeled the ball 20 yards behind him. Not only did he not score, but he cleared the ball away.

RANDOM STUFF

Art—I am honored to know Art. He is an excellent lawyer specializing in contracts law—likely the best in the region, and a very nice guy.

Many years ago, the owner of the Seattle Mariners wanted to move the team out of Seattle.

Local authorities called Art. Art took the owner to court. The team stayed in Seattle.

Years later, the owner of the Seattle Seahawks wanted to move the team out of Seattle.

Local authorities called Art. Art took the owner to court. The team stayed in Seattle.

Years later, the owner of the Seattle Sonics wanted to move the team out of Seattle.

The owner moved the team to Oklahoma.

Why didn't Art keep the Sonics in Seattle like he did the Mariners and the Seahawks?

"My phone didn't ring," says Art. Too bad.

Boring Bill—My kids call my best friend Bill, the guy I have known all my life (and they have known all their lives), "Boring Bill" for some reason. Maybe it is because he does not do dangerous things or his deadpan humor. I think he is the finest man I know (and one of the funniest). He cares more deeply about people than anyone I have ever met.

When Bill was in elementary school and someone hurt themselves. Bill would run over and sympathize with that person. "I am so sorry you are hurt" he would say. I am embarrassed to say I thought at the time that this did not make sense since he was not at fault, and I made fun of him. It just showed how much he cared.

Bill was a bachelor until his late 30s, but he had many friends who recognized what a great catch he would be for the right woman. Bill's humor takes some getting used to. One of the problems with deadpan humor is that it can be mistaken for a strange comment.

Bill was at a party one time and the room was filled with eight people who had known Bill for years, plus Bill and a cute woman Bill was sitting beside. We were all hoping Bill might hit it off with the woman. When Bill turned to her and said, "You are the least ugly person in this room!" there were eight heads that slowly sank into laps. For some reason, the woman did not consider that a compliment.

Dentists—After college I moved back to the Seattle area and needed a dentist as the one I had as a kid had retired. I found one who was a professor at the UW School of Dentistry. I went to get a cavity filled. He gave me a shot of Novocain and started drilling. It hurt a lot and I told him. He gave me another shot. It still hurt a lot. It tried to tell him but he seemed to think two shots was enough. I was white-knuckled, tears streaming down my cheeks. He finally agreed to give me another shot, but he told me it should have been unnecessary. This third shot, into my gums, sprayed into my mouth. His needle had gone all the way through my gums! Let's just say I decided to change dentists.

The next dentist I had for a while, but every time I saw him I got tons of x-rays. He kept talking about his boat. After a while, I figured out that he was maxing out my dental coverage with all those x-rays every six months. Then I heard that one of the girls (now women) on the Chargers soccer team I coached in high school, Sydney Walters, was now a dentist.

Sydney is the best! Based on a small sample, but still.

Tina's Heavy Box—Tina was the girlfriend of a friend. In my opinion, she wore a bit too much makeup, but she was not my girlfriend so I never said anything. I got talked into helping Tina move one day along with several others. I tried to pick up one box about the size of a mini-fridge and it was too heavy for one person to carry. I could tell that it was full to the top of something but it seemed too heavy to be books. I asked Tina what was in the box. A completely full, extra large box of just one thing: Lipstick.

Friend of Franks—One day I bought lunch alone at a Seattle courtyard restaurant with a common seating area and all tables were occupied. I asked if I could share an older woman's table. While we ate, I asked her where she worked. She said she was a psychiatrist. I asked how she got into that. She said it was due to her experience in World War II. She was a prisoner of war. I asked where. She said, "Bergen-Belsen." I knew that was a German concentration camp and I thought I remembered that Anne Frank was a prisoner there. Did she know her? Yes, she knew both Anne and her sister, Margot. They were in an adjacent bunkhouse until they died. She showed me the scar on her arm where she had gotten her arm tattoo removed after the war.

Best reason to become a psychiatrist I ever heard.

I'll bet she is a good psychiatrist. "You think you got problems? You ain't seen nothin'...."

Brake Failure—When we lived in Eastgate, we got a call late at night from our neighbor directly across the street. It seems that our car had rolled down our driveway from our carport in the middle of the night, crossed the street, drove across their front lawn and crashed into their

213

bedroom. We think the emergency brake failed in the middle of the night somehow.

Insurance covered the damage. Several months later, our neighbors decided to put in a new garden. A major feature of their new garden was several giant rocks in the front yard.

Standup Comic Career—My career as a standup comic started on February 12, 1985 at the Comedy Underground in Seattle. My career as a standup comic ended on February 12, 1985 at the Comedy Underground in Seattle.

Jasmine—Our dog Jasmine was the dumbest dog I ever owned. Never got housebroken, ran into things with her head so often we had to have some edges repaired. Once we were walking by a fence listening to a snarling, snapping beast behind it. A hole in the fence about the size of softball was situated such that Jasmine stuck her nose in the hole. Didn't her mom teach her anything? Much blood.

I read an intelligence test somewhere for dogs. Jasmine barely missed getting the lowest score because she knew how to drink from the toilet. However, Jasmine didn't drink so much as eat. Don't think about it.

Tell your children to remember to flush.

Bulldozers—Our first house had a large backyard that was wild and overgrown. It was swampy with a giant old willow tree that had mostly collapsed. I watched one of my neighbors deal with a similar situation in his back yard. He rented a small bulldozer and spent three days using it, taking a vacation day plus a weekend. When he was done, his yard looked pretty nice but my neighbor was tired. He told me that he wished his bulldozer was bigger because he could have been faster. I looked for larger bulldozers, and found one that was about five times as big as the one my neighbor rented. You couldn't rent this bulldozer, you had to hire the guy who owned it. So I did.

In forty-five minutes, my giant tree was gone, I had a nice little creek where my swamp was, and my yard looked better than my neighbor's. I spent less than my neighbor did, too.

Size matters with bulldozers.

Subbing in Softball

—As a kid, I did well in baseball, but didn't play much softball. Once, as an adult I got talked into subbing for someone in softball. I was about 30 years old, but had not played softball since I was a kid. When I got up to bat, the other team moved in close, stepping in front of the bases. I was insulted! They had never seen me play. Why did they think I couldn't hit it out of the infield? I hit the second pitch weakly to the shortstop standing practically next to the pitcher, who threw me out easily. I didn't exactly show them. The next batter came up and they all moved WAY back. The outfield moved back all the way to the fence.

Hey! Why did they think he was so much better than me? I didn't think he looked so special. I was taller than him, too.

The third pitch this guy saw he put not only over the fence, but over the road behind the hill behind the fence. That ball was GONE. No one even went to look for it. The other team could just tell somehow.

Don't ask me to sub for your softball team. But apparently if you play softball, one look at me and you probably won't ask.

Terrible Tree Trimmer

—In Lake Forest Park we lived on a dead end road. If you were to stand on the main street and look into our dead-end street, you would see our neighbor's two-story house to your left, our street in the middle, a 150-foot tree to the right of the road, then a stream to the right of the tree, and farther right was another neighbor's house.

One day a storm knocked over that tree, and it landed across the street on top of our neighbor on the left. The tree had few limbs and had a giant root-ball at the base, so it looked somewhat like a tipped over candle and holder. The neighbor's roof seemed to have relatively little damage for a giant tree falling on it. The road was blocked, and a tree trimmer was called after the storm subsided. I was curious, so I watched him.

The tree trimmer guy started in the middle of the street and sawed downward with a large chainsaw. The chainsaw got stuck. If you think about the physics of that situation, that should not have been a surprise. After getting several more chainsaws stuck, he managed to cut the tree in half, and now the house-side half of the tree caused a lot more damage to the roof as it shifted and fell. He then climbed up on the roof and started sawing, randomly dropping chunks on the roof to roll off and land wherever, with the falling chunks of tree causing more damage to the roof and the house.

Before he started working on the tree leaning on the house, the damage seemed to be confined to the top, "pointy" part of the roof. After he was done, there was lots of damage to the roof, plus the gutters were torn off, plus there was damage to decks where chunks of tree had hit after being cut. Also, the flower beds were now destroyed.

Now that he was done with the house, there was still some tree sticking half-way into the road. He kept cutting off chunks of the tree closer to the base, when suddenly the weight of the root-ball brought the tall stump of the tree back upright. But the tree and root-ball moved about ten feet into the stream, totally blocking the stream. The newly blocked stream started flooding the neighbor's house on the right.

Mr. Terrible Tree Trimmer then left.

My neighbor on the right, who previously had no damage, now had a flooded house. He had to hire TWO tow trucks (one alone could not move the tree) to pull the tree out of the stream so his house would stop flooding.

Dented Civic—A friend of mine drove his Honda Civic to Fairbanks on the Alaska Highway, which is a 1400 mile mostly gravel road through northern Canada to Alaska. When he got there, someone asked him why his car had so many dents on all four sides. Because he hit a moose going about 60 mph, he said. That explains the front, but what about the other three sides? The moose was pissed off, and kicked the car for half an hour.

Land Lines—We got rid of our land line phone a few years ago. Going "all internet" was cheaper and we got to keep our old phone number, which was important. Then, we had a problem. For a small business, having your customers hear "Sorry, that line has been disconnected" means that customer is almost surely lost forever. Who tries a disconnected line later to see if it has been reconnected? That problem needs to be fixed as fast as possible.

We found out that by state law, if you have a problem like this with an "all internet" service, they have to refund your money, but they don't have to fix it. We went 30 days before we found out they didn't have to fix it. If you have a problem like this with a land line, by state law they have 72 hours to fix it.

We reconnected our land line. The phone number is still 425-821-5529. Call if you have a great story.

Lost Ring—One of the neighborhood kids—about four years old at the time—was at our house one day and told us, "If anyone finds a wedding ring, it is probably my dad's. He threw his out the window yesterday."

About two months later, those neighbors divorced.

Saw that coming.

Sprough and Squirrels—Our beagle dog Sprough had a collar that jangled. It made it easy to tell where he was. He loved to chase squirrels but never caught one. One day we were out in the woods and there was something wrong with his collar. I took it off for a second to work on it. Almost immediately, Sprough caught a squirrel.

Pool Removal—When we bought our house in Kirkland, it had a heated, above-ground pool. The weather in the Seattle area is rarely hot enough for a pool. For example, on average the temperature exceeds 90 just three times per year in our area. As a result, we did not use the pool often. We also had (and still have) a hot tub, which we use much more often. I calculated one day that the pool cost us almost $3 per use (due largely to all the maintenance in the fall-winter-spring) while the hot tub cost us about 25 cents per use.

One day, a dog who chased something onto the pool cover ripped it and the pool liner getting out. We decided to take the pool out rather than fix it. A friend of ours borrowed his company's dump truck one Saturday and we loaded up the aluminum pieces of the pool (aside from the cover and liner, which we tossed, it was all aluminum) into the dump truck and drove to a place that paid for surplus aluminum. We pulled into the empty parking lot at 2 pm. The sign on the door said they closed at 1 pm on Saturdays and were closed on Sundays.

I turned to my friend and asked, "What are we going to do now?"

He didn't say anything. He just pushed a button and I heard the truck start to dump its load.

Mount St. Helens Erupts—[Cousin Rick] We were in bed asleep in our house in Lake Forrest Park, north of Seattle, when Lorraine and I sat bolt upright at the exact time Mount St. Helen erupted, 160 miles or so south of us. What was that noise?

Boston Cop—As mentioned earlier, there appear to be far more police on the roads in the state of Washington than we saw in other states. The local police are pretty serious about laws. For example, I know two people who have gotten jaywalking tickets in Seattle. One person decided not to pay his ticket and ended up in jail. Some laws like this do not seem to be enforced in other states, I guess.

We were in Boston wanting to cross a six-lane, busy street to go to a park. We had a child in a stroller. The nearest intersection had no marked crosswalk. The nearest marked crosswalk appeared to be about ¼ mile away. I asked a cop how we should cross the street. The cop sarcastically said, "You want to cross the street? So CROSS the STREET!"

Best of Seattle—It seems that every "ten best things to do in Seattle" list includes "Visit Victoria, BC" as though that was something to do in Seattle. However, I was in Victoria one day and overheard a tourist asking a local about the ten best things to do in Victoria: Sure enough "Visit Seattle" was near the top of their list.

Molly—In high school I was in certain "upper level" classes—math, English, etc. It was typically the same 20 or so kids in these classes. Years after high school, one girl named Molly from these classes I heard got in trouble with the law. She was a stockbroker who was accused of taking money from her clients. I read about this in the news and wanted to hear her side of the story so I arranged to meet her for lunch. At lunch Molly seemed unconcerned. She had merely "borrowed" the money and would pay it back. I was wondering to myself how she would pay it back as the news said she had been fired and fined, likely to go to prison plus was expected to pay restitution plus expensive legal fees, when she interrupted my thought process by asking me for a loan.

Let me think about that. I am done thinking about that. No.

Paving with Larry—Lorraine was asked by a friend who worked on a paving crew one day if she would flag—that is, hold up the "Stop/Slow" sign while the crew was paving. She did, and soon Lorraine was paving, too. I joked that she started to leave the toilet seat up at home.

Except for Lorraine the entire crew was guys in their late 20s and early 30s including one guy named Larry. Lorraine noticed that when lunchtime came around, Larry always got his lunch at the nearest 7-11 or convenience store, and lunch every day for Larry consisted of Twinkies, Ho-Hos, Doritos, a Snickers bar and a large sugary drink. Lorraine, who made sure our entire family ate vegetables every day, was disgusted.

About four years after Lorraine quit paving, she heard that Larry had died of some kind of stomach or intestinal problem before the age of 40.

I'll keep eating those vegetables, thank you.

Stop/Slow Signs—Twice now I have been traveling through a construction zone and a flagger with one of those signs that says STOP on one side and SLOW on the other, has frantically waived their arms at me shouting "Stop! Stop!" while showing the SLOW side of his sign.

I am only going to explain this job ONE MORE TIME....

State Inspector—[Cousin Rick] I had a friend who had a job where

he was supposed to sit and watch someone doing something in a food processing plant and press the stop button if the person fell into a bin. He said it was the most boring job in the world, so everyone who had the job mostly read books or played games. He said he got bored with his book one day, so he decided to do just exactly what he was supposed to be doing, which was watching his co-worker with his hand on the stop button in case he fell in.

The state inspector came in for a surprise inspection. The inspector was very upset, because he had always before fined the company for the person not doing the safety job. The inspector was certain my friend had been tipped off, somehow. Nope, just coincidence.

Coffee Filters—One day we were at my sister's house with my

cousin Rick, and Rick had to go to the bathroom. My sister told my Rick that she was out of toilet paper, but she had lots of coffee filters. Rick's response: "Doesn't that make the coffee taste funny?"

I Remember You—I happened to be driving by my old elementary

school one day. I was in my early 40s. I stopped to see if there were any teachers I recognized. Since it had been nearly forty years since I had attended, there was only one teacher left who was there when I was. She had been my third grade teacher, and was in her early 20s when I had her, now in her 60s. I asked if she remembered me. At first, she didn't.

Then she said, "Now I remember you! Funny-looking bald kid!"

I should have kept driving.

Attention Environmentalists—Use your favorite search engine and look up "Colorado Big Thompson Project." I am amazed that few environmentalists seem to care about this huge, ongoing environmental disaster. Coal plants—Colorado has 14 (Washington and Oregon have one each)—are providing power to pump water from the Colorado River—essentially stealing water from California farmers—under a national park to the Platte River to benefit Nebraska farmers. The official map of Rocky Mountain National Park shows—faintly—how the giant water-stealing tunnel goes under one side of the park to the other. And people get all worked up about plastic straws!

Hiding Baldness—Since about age eight I have had basically the same hairstyle—combed from left to right on the top of my head. Now that I am bald, and there is little hair to comb. When I first started going bald, however, I was often accused of "trying to hide" my baldness by combing my hair the way I always combed it. "That comb-over is not fooling anyone" is among the idiotic statements I heard. I did "That comb-over" for 25 years, buddy, and suddenly I am hiding something? I am convinced that no matter what a guy does when he is going bald short of shaving everything, he is accused of "trying to hide it" by inconsiderate clods. Maybe I was just surrounded by inconsiderate clods when I was in my early 30s? Nah. Going bald is attractive...to inconsiderate clods and stupid remarks.

Golfing with Greg—I hadn't seen my poker buddy Greg for a while when we reconnected at a high school reunion. We decided to get together to play golf. Greg got a foursome together including me at his favorite course.

When I got there, I was introduced to the other two players of the foursome, which were the owner of the golf course and the owner's son. As we walked toward the pro shop, it seemed like more people knew Greg than knew either the owner or her son. Of course, no one knew me. Greg was a big hit everywhere. People went out of their way to come over and shake his hand. It was difficult to start playing, because so many people stopped to greet mostly Greg and to some extent the owner. As we approached the first tee, a woman driving a cart with beverages came up to us. She jumped out of her cart and gave Greg a big hug, and said she had his favorite liqueur for him. He ordered a Vente coffee (largest size) with a sizeable shot of that liqueur. I bought a diet Coke.

As we finished the second hole and started toward the third tee, the beverage lady came by again. I was fine as I had taken maybe two sips from my drink. Greg ordered another Vente coffee with liqueur.

As we finished the fourth hole, the beverage lady came by again. I had taken a few more sips, but still had more than half my drink left. Greg ordered a beer.

As we got to the seventh tee, the beverage lady came by again. By this time I had finished almost exactly half of my drink, so I was fine. Greg was on the tee, so she waited quietly for him to finish before asking him if he wanted anything. I whispered to her, "Do you really think he wants another drink?" She whispered back, "If he doesn't order something it will be the first time ever." Sure enough, after teeing off Greg ordered another beer.

The eighth hole was a long par five, and my ball was close to Greg's in the middle of the fairway (his in one shot, mine in three—I am not a great golfer). Greg was a bit tipsy by this point, and I was wondering where he was putting all that liquid. Suddenly, in the middle of the fairway, he decided to pee, in full view of the owner and her son and anyone else. Nobody said a thing.

Although Greg was wobbling a bit by this point, he managed to get his second shot barely on the front edge of the green, with about a 100-foot putt. Minutes later, we all watched Greg sway as he sank that 100-foot putt for an eagle.

I guess the moral of this story is that if you are a celebrity you can pee wherever you want.

Dan's Plan—Another friend from my elementary school soccer team I ran into as an adult is Dan. Dan is a painter with a plan. He found many subcontractors—electricians, framers, plumbers, etc.—and offered to paint their houses for free if they agreed to help him build a house some day. They agreed. He found everyone he needed except a Mason. When the time came, Dan had a beautiful house built using a whole lot of favors, plus one hired Mason for his fireplace and chimney.

Learning From a Fourth-Grader—When I was new to Facebook, I accepted a friend's daughter's "friend request." Bree was a fourth-grader at the time. Nice girl. Next thing I know, my Facebook page has lots of photos of ten-year-old girls in pajamas taken at Bree's sleepover.

What have I done?

In general, older men have trouble explaining why they feature photos of ten-year-old girls in pajamas who are not family members on their Facebook feed. Not saying there is anything wrong, just awkward to explain. I didn't want to "unfriend" her.

Lesson from a fourth-grader: Just because someone is a friend and a nice person does not necessarily mean you want their photos on your Facebook feed.

New Shower Door—One day our glass shower door broke. We had to shower behind a plastic curtain—can you imagine how awful it is to shower behind a plastic curtain rather than a glass shower door? I know, it is hard to even imagine.

A few days later I sat next to someone I had never met at a networking lunch who said he was a contractor. I asked him if he could fix our glass shower door. He said he could. The next day he came over to our house, took some measurements, put all our door hardware into a white bag and left, saying he would be back in a week to replace the door. One week later, I called him and he said it would be another week. After another week went by, all my new calls to this guy went directly to voice mail. I kept calling every few days—always voice mail. Finally, three weeks later, I realized I only had his phone number, and I would have to look up his physical address to contact him. When I Googled his name, the first result was an obit. The guy had died! And then he refused to answer my calls! I had to play detective—where was that white bag with my door hardware? His sister looked in his apartment and his truck and did not find it. I called several glass companies that made glass shower doors, and on my third call—bingo! "Yeah, some guy left a white bag with hardware in it here a few weeks ago and never picked up the door he ordered."

Upset Bus Driver—I used to ride the 257 bus every day to and from work about 12 miles from Kirkland to Seattle and back. One day, a sign at my normal downtown bus stop said the bus stop was closed and to wait one block north. There were seven who normally rode the 257 waiting one block north of the normal stop per the directions on the sign when our 257 bus went by without stopping. Since our 257 bus came every 45 minutes, we didn't want to wait for the next bus if possible. Six people ran north trying to catch the bus at the next stop, about four blocks away. I got on the local 18 bus that happened to be there—not the correct bus, but I knew it would go in the correct direction for about 10 blocks. I asked the 18 bus driver to call the 257 bus driver and ask him to wait at the next stop for several people he failed to pick up. The 18 bus driver talked into his handset for a few moments, then turned pale. He told me in a voice that was both apologetic and confused, "He said no."

As it turned out due to traffic and lights, the 18 bus pulled up behind the 257 about 10 blocks up the street. I ran out of the 18 and onto the 257. I quietly said to the bus driver that he had missed some folks at one stop. He said that he was running late and could not wait.

Oh, well, I thought. At least I made the bus. I sat down and started to read the newspaper.

There were two more stops in Seattle and people got on as normal, then the bus headed out as normal for the 12 mile journey to Kirkland with two mid-point stops. After about 10 miles, the bus pulled into a Park and Ride it normally did not serve. The driver stopped the bus, stood and faced the riders and yelled, "I am sick and tired of everyone bugging me!" He then went outside to a bench, sat down and angrily crossed his arms. Awkward. The riders slowly got off the bus, all staring at me because nobody else had talked to the bus driver. Another bus came by a few moments later and picked us up to take us the last two miles.

"My Fault" Accidents—[Cousin Rick] In forty-plus years of driving, I have been in a number of accidents. I don't think any of the accidents were my fault, but insurance companies don't agree. Three of the accidents I have had over the years were deemed to be entirely my fault by the insurance agencies. You decide.

The first one I was driving a big van full of our family in Canada on the TransCanada highway. The road was mostly one lane in each direction, but we had just gone up an incline. The speed limit was 60 mph and that is what everyone was going. There were a lot of cars. As we got to the top of the incline and started to go downhill, we came upon a sign that said the right lane would end in 500 meters (about a third of a mile). I was in the left lane as was the car ahead of me as we were passing a large truck in the right lane at 60 mph. The car ahead of me slammed on her brakes. The pavement was wet, and I skidded into her. It turned out that the driver was 16 years old, and was worried about the truck (who had made no movement or signal from his lane), so chose to stop in the highway from 60 mph to zero. Per the insurance companies, it was entirely my fault as I hit her from behind. I could not dodge left as oncoming lane was busy, and the right lane had a truck in it, so I had little choice. The collision shop where we got our van fixed said I skidded so much tread off my tire, that he estimated that I must have skid for about a quarter mile. That sounded about right to me. No one in either vehicle seemed to be injured at the time, but I am told the folks in the car later claimed injury when talking to my insurance company. Entirely my fault. Sigh.

The second one was I was driving on a freeway where there were two lanes going in the same direction eastbound with a third exit lane where traffic was stopped. In the two lanes where traffic was moving, speed limit was 60 mph and most cars were doing that. I was in the lane next to the stopped traffic, which made me nervous, so I was going about 45 mph. A car jumped out of the stopped line in front of me and I hit them from behind, and since I hit them from behind it was entirely my fault. Sigh.

The third time was when I was backing out of my driveway. A car driven by a teenage boy a few doors down hit me in my driveway. Since I was backing up, the boy's insurance company claimed it was entirely my fault because I was close to the road, even though I was in my own driveway. Sigh.

In this third case, at least my insurance company disagreed.

Vivien and Friends—Our family signed up for house exchanges

because we found this was a great way to vacation with a large family. As you know, Lorraine and I have four daughters. The way exchanges were done before the internet is that you paid for an ad in a big book of people all over the world interested in exchanges. Then, you found someone in the book who lived where you wanted to go, and you contacted them by mail. Usually you exchanged houses, but you could offer anything.

One day I got a letter from Vivien from Switzerland, who was a college student planning to travel to the Seattle area with two friends and wondered if the three of them could sleep for one night on couches in our basement for free (in the ad you describe your house, so they knew we had couches in our basement). They didn't have much money and it was okay if I said no. I thought one night was not a big deal, so I wrote back and said okay. When the day and time arrived, I opened my door to find three six-foot plus Swiss guys. It did not occur to me that Vivien and friends might be males. It all worked out fine, but my young daughters were confused, as I had told them three college girls would be staying.

Marathon—Since I had run cross country and track in high school and

then kept up my running in college and after, I decided that I should try a marathon. At the time I decided to do this, I was running about five miles per night (I always ran at night), and I would always go with my dog Sprough. I started working my way up to six miles per night, then seven, etc. When I got to ten miles per night, all of the sudden Sprough, rather than being excited when I got my running shoes on, stopped wanting to run with me.

I had worked my way up to seventeen miles per night when the day of the marathon came. I was in good shape, and I was running pretty hard.

There were a lot of people. It took almost 45 seconds to get to the starting line after the gun sounded, but we were off. I did the first ten miles in less than one hour (that is fast!), and I was met at this point by my friend John from high school who I ran cross country with. John helped me keep a good pace up until about mile 20, when the wind picked up, and I started running directly into the wind. When you are working on mile 21, running against the wind is tough. I looked up and I could see about twelve people ahead of me, all walking. John saw me look and said "No way, Rough!" He would not let me walk. The last five miles were the hardest. About 800 yards from the finish line, John peeled off, and I finished with a respectable 3:19. Ask any marathoner. That is a pretty good time.

You don't know tired until you have run a marathon. I decided that was the last time I would do a marathon. But see below.

Another Marathon—My daughter Amanda decided she was going to run a marathon, and invited Lorraine and I to watch. I remembered how much I appreciated John running the last 16 miles with me, so I decided to run the last, uh...ahem...six miles with Amanda. It was raining that day, and rather than stand in the rain wearing running gear, I stood with a raincoat and umbrella, with the running gear underneath. We were not sure when she would get there, so we got there early, to the 20 mile mark at the base of a long hill.

After about 45 minutes, I saw her. By the time I ran to the car and put the raincoat and umbrella in it, she had run past and was about a quarter mile up the hill I was at the base of.

I ran to quickly catch up to her. As I flew by a couple of marathoners, one slowly said "heeyyy, wait-a-minute" in a tone that clearly indicated that he didn't believe I had just run 20 miles.

Like John, my plan was to peel off before the end. Unlike John, I was unable to do so, as there were a bunch of folks "helping" me to the finish line (pushing me toward the line) because I was so close it would be a shame for me to stop. I ended up crossing the finish line with a little help a few seconds behind my daughter although that was not my intent. Somebody put a medal around my neck and shook my hand. A photographer took my picture. I felt bad a little. I did not intend to cheat, just to support my daughter.

MBA—When I had been at SCL for less than two years, I signed up at the University of Washington (UW) for a masters degree in Electrical Engineering. This was the same year our first child Amanda was born, and the UW did not have a night program at the time. This meant I would go to work early, take a bus to the UW for two classes, then take the bus back to SCL, and work late. Then I had to do homework on top of that. I decided it was too much, with a new baby and all. I ended up dropping out of the program after just two classes, but I did get a 3.9 out of a possible 4.0 grade point average for those two classes.

Twenty-six years later, when I had been at SCL for 28 years, they started a tuition reimbursement program if an employee entered a masters degree program. I jumped at the chance and signed up for a masters in business administration (MBA) at UW Bothell campus, just a few miles from my house. My application was sent in to UW past the normal deadline, but someone cancelled and I got in because of my existing cumulative 3.9 grade point average!

It was tough work. Classes were at night, 5:45 to 10:15 two nights a week, plus homework. For the first time in my life, I left a party we were invited to on a Saturday night after less than an hour because I had homework!

I had fun, though. When a professor asked me for an example of "Unearned Revenue" I suggested charging students for tuition before classes start. When the accounting professor asked for an example of overhead at the UW I suggested the lights in the room.

What was less fun was the fact that SCL decided to cancel the tuition reimbursement program (for everyone) after only one quarter. So, I had a choice of quitting or continuing on my own dime.

I didn't quit. I liked it. We had top-level executives from Nordstrom, Boeing, Google, and Starbucks come to class to lecture and in some cases to critique our work. I enjoyed the students I worked with as well. It was fun when twice during "up-beat" presentations from large well-known businesses, students found data that contradicted the presentation. How dare we prove their marketing was wrong?

My GPA ended up being 3.7 for the MBA, but I think it really should have been lower. Twice, professors handed assignments back to me and told me to "hand this in tomorrow." I got the hint to redo it, because both times others were not told this and I noticed that the assignments being turned in were, uh, a lot better than mine.

(I wished *My Friend Tom* had had these professors).

My final project was working on a marketing plan for a local company that does clinical testing for biopharmaceuticals. It turned out that compared to their competition, the company I was trying to help was somewhat faster because they had fewer steps, yet ended up with the same end product as their competition. I suggested that in their advertising they use a jar of peanut butter to represent their company, and a bag of peanuts to represent their competition, and both processes end up with a peanut butter sandwich. In my presentation, for drama I dumped a big bag of unshelled peanuts on their conference table. I was told that there were still unshelled peanuts on that conference table six months later.

Moclips—We bought a timeshare on the Washington coast in the tiny town of Copalis Beach one year. It was a one-sixth share, which meant we got to use the unit every six weeks. I think we almost never missed going out to Copalis Beach when it was our time.

One weekend we were staying at our timeshare and we decided to go to a garage sale. The house was for sale, too. I asked the price. It was an oceanfront house for $104,000. In Seattle, waterfront of any kind started at well over a million dollars, so I was amazed at how cheap that sounded. We didn't buy the garage sale house, but we started looking. Besides, my investments in the stock market were not performing at the time, so real estate sounded like a better bet to me.

We found a duplex in Moclips, WA. We eventually bought it. It came with a buildable lot next door. We then sold the timeshare.

Whoever decorated the duplex may have been on drugs at the time. It had purple shag carpet in the kitchen, blue astro-turf in the bedroom, orange industrial carpet in the living room, striped ceilings, beaded doorways, bright pink flowery wallpaper, and a round window with a wide wooden frame that probably was supposed to look like a porthole but actually looked more like a toilet seat.

In spite of the beautiful decor, we remodeled.

We started calling it the RoughHouse.org Cabin. The web site, not surprisingly, is www.roughhouse.org.

We were exited that we got four renters in a row when we first started to rent the Cabin. The three later rentals were all renting at the end of road trips, so we gave all four parties duplicate keys so there would be no hassles later. We thought. The very first renter locked his keys inside, so rather than call us or a neighbor, he called a locksmith. This was NOT "The Subtle Locksmith"—he sawed off the doorknob and installed a new one, which required a NEW KEY. We then had to get a copy of this new key, quickly copy it, and get keys to the other renters somehow plus the cleaners all from where we were 180 miles away. The first renter then asked for a discount because he bought us a new doorknob. No.

Someone in my MBA class pointed out that I should not have the fun story of a nearby skunk family on the web site. In hindsight, that seems like a pretty obvious story to leave off the web site. You don't want to be known as the place that is near the place that "does not smell bad anymore."

For almost ten years I looked at that buildable lot next to the Cabin and finally took the plunge and decided to build. One of the guys on my soccer team, the Shamrocks, was a contractor who agreed to build the "R&R House" I designed for the lot next door. On a couple of weekends I invited a bunch of Shamrocks out to the ocean to help. It is amazing how fast a contractor can work when he has ten guys carrying lumber for him.

The R&R House web site is www.RetreatsAndReunions.com or www.randrhouse.com

R&R House on the left, RoughHouse.org Cabin on the right taken while standing in the ocean.

We realized after owning both the Cabin and the R&R House that we always stayed at the R&R House and ended up working on the Cabin, which always needed fixing up. Neither one was a big money-maker. The main value was being able to stay at a place you owned. Big and new is more fun than small and old. At least with us. We sold the Cabin in August 2019. I wonder if the new owners will see the pink flowery wallpaper in the bedroom closet and realize that the entire Cabin once had that wallpaper.

First R&R Rental— Next to the RoughHouse.org Cabin we had owned for almost ten years in Moclips I built a big house with the help of guys on the Shamrocks soccer team. I called it the "R&R House" and the web site is www.RetreatsAndReunions.com. We all worked extra hard to get it ready for the very first rental on the popular July 4 weekend. I was excited to have two properties side-by-side so that large groups could rent both properties or two smaller groups could each rent one.

I was excited by all the possibilities. I met the first R&R House renter arriving for the July 4 weekend. He drove in towing a large flatbed trailer. I wondered what he had in the trailer since I told him that we had all the linens and bedding he might need. He told me the trailer was full of fireworks. Fireworks were legal on the beach and he planned a four-hour show.

I also greeted the cabin renter who arrived moments later. She said that she lived in an area where there were too many fireworks and so she came out to the ocean to enjoy a quiet July 4 weekend.

My comment: "Good luck!"

Deposit—We hold a deposit when someone rents one of our units. Once we see that there has been no damage, we return the deposit. We have found that our renters take better care of things when a deposit is involved.

One time, a couple rented our place, just the two of them, for a romantic oceanfront weekend. Rather than giving us a deposit, the woman gave us her diamond wedding ring to hold as a deposit. Her husband did not seem to mind. Or, I should say, the man she was with did not seem to mind.

Kidney Stones and Cheese—I suddenly had horrible pain at

work one day. I could hardly stand up. One of the people I work with took me to the ER and it turned out that I had a kidney stone. Unbelievably painful. They said at the ER they were not going to do anything about it except give me pain medication and wait for it to pass. I got a shot of the strong stuff for pain, but I needed more. I ended up setting a record for pain shots. I took ten. The previous record was eight. After I had had nine shots, I asked for one more. The nurse said I should be asleep. I said I would love to be asleep.

I have great new respect for moms.

A month later, I had another kidney stone. I repeated the incredible pain, but went to a specialist to see what could be done about not having another. The doctor ran lots of tests, and seemed frustrated. He then ran some more, but didn't have a good answer. After his third set of tests, he said to me, "Do you sometimes go for months without eating cheese and then eat about seven pieces of pizza?" I said, "yes, I do." He said, "Well, cut it out!" (I hate cheese and never eat it, except mozzarella on pizza).

According to the doctor, my problem could be boiled down to cheese, or concentrated calcium. He told me to not eat more than one slice of pizza per day, or two yogurts, or three bowls of ice cream, or five glasses of milk. I did what he said and over 20 years later I have not had another kidney stone.

Someone once told me that the sense of taste was originally supposed to be to keep you from eating poison. I hate cheese, and my body tells me it is poison. Others might disagree.

Targeted Marketing—I hate targeted marketing on the internet. This was started by Amazon. At one point, the only two things I bought on Amazon were a Broadway hits CD for my aunt, and rat poison. Afterwards, "People who bought those things also bought…." Yeah, right.

My Mom's Best Friend—My mom had died decades earlier, but we are still in touch with her best friend, whom I drove home from church one Easter. At 92 years old she still owns a car. Her sons took away her keys, saying she could Uber the occasional trip to the store or to church. Her sons drove her everywhere else. Don't tell her sons, but I think she has a hidden car key. Anyway, as I loaded her rather large bag into my trunk, I wondered how good her memory was at the age of 92, so I asked her a few subtle questions on the five-minute ride to her house. She seemed fine, but it was hard to be sure. Then, as I helped her to her door, she turned and said, "don't forget my bag." I had forgotten her bag.

She's fine.

Lizzie Graduates From Gonzaga—My cousin's daughter Lizzie's real name is Elisabeth and her mom is Lisa. We went to see Lizzie graduate. So, when I got to the hotel I said, "I'd like to check in for my daughter Lisa Rough--her real name is Elizabeth Rough--but there is already a Lisa Rough and an Elisabeth Rough here." The clerk asked, 'Is she rooming with Carolyn?" and I said "Bingo!"

The commencement speaker said he often has the following exchange when he tells folks on the East Coast that he is from Gonzaga University:

Where is that? Spokane

Where is that? Washington

DC? No Washington State

You went to Washington State?

Parking Pass—Some friends gave us a flyer they bought at a charity auction good for parking at four mutually agreed upon Seattle Sounders games, since we own season tickets to the Sounders and our friends did not. The flyer had an address near the stadium and contact info, but no directions. I emailed the person on the flyer telling him what days we wanted and did not get a response. So, on the day of the first game we had chosen, we drove to the address and could not figure out what to do. We could not find an obvious place to park. So, we went to the parking garage next to the address and handed them the flyer. They shrugged and let us park for free. Two days later, we got an email that was all apologetic that they had not responded sooner. I told them what we had done. They said that was not correct, and told us where the parking spot actually was. The following game we parked correctly and we ended up meeting the guy who donated the parking flyer. He was very nice.

I am considering printing up "charity parking flyers" to hand to other parking garages near the stadium. Might work.

Oprah Winfrey—Speaking of things that just might work, for the same reason that I have put Cousin Rick in this book every once in a while, I thought I would mention Oprah Winfrey. Did you know that Erik Logan and Sheri Salata are Co-Presidents at HARPO, Inc., the company that Oprah Winfrey founded? Might work.

Fireworks Injury—On July 4, 2005 I was shooting off fireworks, and some neighbor kids asked if we had a particular kind of firework. Yes, I said, and I opened our sliding glass door, literally ran out to our shed, grabbed the firework, and ran back, breaking my nose on the now closed sliding door, which I did not see or expect to be closed. Lorraine had closed it behind me without telling me.

I used my broken nose as a teaching moment for my kids: "See kids? Fireworks can cause injuries."

A Pig Valve—I was playing on two soccer teams and running about
three to five miles per day at the age of 49, and was in pretty good shape. One day I decided to run even though I had the flu. Having the flu did not usually keep me from running. My run was all uphill, so I was a bit more out of breath than usual. The next day, I was still out of breath. That was odd, but I thought the flu might be the cause. The next day happened to be Christmas Eve 2005, and although my flu symptoms had lessened, I was still out of breath. I started to run one of those symptom checkers on the internet, and it stopped after a few questions and insisted I go straight to the doctor. Due to the timing, that meant the Emergency Room, and I thought I would wait until after festivities on Christmas Day, which I did. I told my sister that my plan was to go to the ER after Christmas breakfast. She said her food wasn't *that* bad.

At the ER, they misdiagnosed (as it turned out) that I had pneumonia, gave me some antibiotics and told me to see my regular doctor the next day if I didn't get better.

I didn't get better, so I went to see my regular doctor, who spent two hours running tests, finally threw up her hands and said she didn't know what was going on and sent me back to the ER. At the ER this time was a group of cardiac students being taught by two instructors, who diagnosed heart failure.

Heart failure? Say what? I was running several miles per day, playing soccer, etc. What are you talking about? Well, according to their tests, one of my heart valves had failed. That was odd, because in July of that year, when I had broken my nose, the nurse who treated me said that she

238

used to be a cardiac nurse and she told me that she could tell that my heart valves were fine, except that I probably had a bicuspid valve (About 2% of the people in the world have a bicuspid valve, and most never know since it does not usually have any symptoms). She also said that heart valves take years to fail. So how did my valve fail after only a few months?

They didn't know how it failed so fast. They told me I needed to set up surgery to have a replacement valve put in my heart. I did some research with a friend in the medical field and we found the best surgeon to do heart valve replacements. However, he was on vacation, due to return in 11 days. I reluctantly got on his schedule for surgery in 11 days.

They did a surgical procedure where they thread a tiny video camera through an artery in your leg up into my heart to have a look. After they saw the results, they told me I would not live for 11 days—two at the most—and I had to have surgery first thing in the morning. I asked if there was room on the surgery schedule tomorrow morning and they said they schedule based on greatest need. That was me. Did I consent to have surgery in the morning? I said give me a minute to think. The doctor went out in the hall.

I am told my sister, who had been told all this already, grabbed the doctor by the lapels in the hall and said, "Talk him into it!"

I had two decisions to make quickly—should I have major open-heart surgery tomorrow? Not really a choice, I would die if I didn't. The second decision was equally important—should I get a pig valve or a mechanical valve? If I got a pig valve, it would be expected to last about 15 to 20 years (11 as it turned out, see below), but if I got a mechanical valve it would last for the rest of my life. With the pig valve, I could continue normal activities, because I would not need to be on any special medications. With the mechanical valve, I would have to be on blood thinners for the rest of my life, and could no longer play soccer, jog, bike and hike. That, too, was not really a decision. Soccer, jogging, biking and hiking were too big a part of my life.

The other good thing about the pig valve is that researchers had been working on a procedure where in the not too distant future, a pig valve could be replaced with minor surgery, the kind where you go in through an artery in your leg like they did with the tiny camera.

So, I decided on the pig valve.

I fully expected to die on the operating table.

I was so excited to wake up after surgery. I didn't die! I tend to be a bit of a wiseacre, and I started to give the nurse attending me a hard time, just because I was so happy to be alive! She told me, "The reason I like to work in this unit is that the patients don't usually TALK!" I was out of her unit in less than ten minutes.

However, it soon became apparent that although I didn't die, my heart was getting worse. I had a very high fever. The surgeon had decided to have my old heart valve biopsied, and it turned out I had an incredibly rare bacteria. A study done in the 1980s found only 34 cases of this type of bacteria in the history of the world! This bacteria, called "cardio bacterium hominus," was eating my heart. Replacing the valve had not stopped it. It was still eating my heart and in two more days, enough of my heart would be destroyed that I would need an entire new heart.

The reason it is so rare is that in order to have cardio bacterium hominus attack your heart, you need to have:

1) the bacterium in your body (doctors don't know how it gets in your body or where it comes from),
2) a bicuspid heart valve (which I did),
3) a recent tiny tear in the valve (these happen naturally and virtually always repair themselves in about two weeks), and
4) the flu.

Having the flu somehow activates the bacterium. I lucked out I guess.

Vancomycin, the strongest antibiotic doctors normally use, did not work against this rare bacteria. Plus, as it turned out, I was allergic to vancomycin. They had to do some original research at the University of Washington Medical Center to find out what worked against this rare bacteria. The only thing that worked? Plain old penicillin.

The doctors decided to put a plastic line into my arm and thread it though my arteries into my heart, and drip penicillin into my heart for six weeks. They told me that six weeks was probably far longer than needed, as the penicillin appeared to have killed the bacteria after only a week, but the only way they could tell the bacteria was still alive was by having my heart start to fail again.

Here is an actual quote from the technician during the procedure to put this plastic line in my arteries from my arm to my heart, while the technician and I were both watching the line snake slowly along on an x-ray video screen of my body: "It is really hard making the corner right after your shoulder toward your heart. I keep going into your brain! Sorry."

Due to how unusual my situation was, the doctors sent me to the woman who "wrote the book on cardiology" in that she was the author of the textbook on cardiology that pretty much every cardiology medical student in the US studies. She happens to live in the Seattle area and so I was sent to see her. She pretty much told me the same story that all other cardiologists told. I was a rare guy.

After a week of the penicillin drip, I started to get better. After I healed from the surgery, I appeared to be fine.

Fine, except that we found out later the pig valve put into my heart was too small. This is a problem for two reasons, 1. This means that the new procedure to replace the valve via a leg artery will not work, because that procedure must replace the valve with an even smaller valve because it does everything inside of a single artery, and 2. See *DWTS Saves My Life* below.

I nearly died #7.

DWTS Saves My Life—On April 17, 2017, I accidently died. I
didn't mean to. Doctors said it was not a heart attack. A heart attack is
when gunk in or near your heart stops your heart. I had no gunk. That's
good, right? I had a "Sudden Death Event." Oh.

I was exercising as usual at the local 24 Hour Fitness. I exercise harder
than most. I was using the Stairmaster this day. When I last did the
Stairmaster, I had done 200 flights. That is a lot—that is like climbing the
three tallest buildings in Seattle. On this day, I did 130 flights and was
quite tired. Only two buildings. I thought I could do ten more floors, but
it was much more difficult than usual. I was frustrated because I thought I
should be able to do even more, but I stopped at 140 flights. I went to my
wife on an elliptical machine and said I was tired and wanted to leave—I
was driving—but she wanted to watch the rest of "Dancing with the
Stars" (DWTS). Ok, so now what? Even though I was tired, I decided to
get on the elliptical machine next to my wife. From my perspective at this
point, they turned out the lights.

From the story I heard (I was "not there"), a random guy who normally
works at a casino named Steven Charie—now my hero—was using a
nearby machine and heard a crash. I had started to collapse into the
elliptical machine. I had gone stiff and was exhaling. He and my wife tried
to grab me. After about 15 seconds, I collapsed into the elliptical
machine. Steven, Lorraine and a couple of others extracted me and laid
me on my back. Steven started CPR and timed it (!) for 2.5 minutes.
While doing compressions, he asked a gym staffer if they had a
defibrillator. "Uh, yeah" said the otherwise silent and unmoving staffer
nearby, and went to get it. Steven said I looked dead. Blue face, not
breathing. He didn't think I would make it. He hooked up the
defibrillator, and the machine said a shock was indicated. The machine
said to tell all bystanders to stay back and press the button for a shock.
The gym staffer said, "I'm not pressing that button." Steven said, "It said

press the button, I'm going to press the button!" and did. The shock caused my body to come completely off the floor. Per instructions from the machine, Steven did a few more seconds of CPR.

From my perspective, the lights came back on at this point.

No white lights, no tunnels, no angels. Just lights off, then lights on.

I saw a guy I now know was Steven Charie pull back and four EMTs close in on me, putting a stretcher to my right. Behind the EMTs were about a half-dozen people wearing sweaty t-shirts and shocked expressions. One of the EMTs asked me how I was feeling. As noted earlier, I have always been a wiseacre. I realized what must have happened, so I said, "Well, I guess I'll be going home now."

The EMT laughed, and said, no, "you are going with us!" Another EMT stepped on my left foot at this point. OUCH! I almost put myself onto the stretcher reacting to getting my foot stepped on. They gave me an IV, then loaded me into the back of the van, and they took me lights and sirens (bells and whistles) to Evergreen Hospital. On the way, the guy in the back with me said, "You look WAY better than the average guy we haul." I took that as a compliment.

As soon as I got to Evergreen Hospital, they rushed me into surgery to put one of those cameras into one of my arteries to look at my heart. Using this, along with some other tests, they determined that I had no oxygen deprivation damage. None! It was all due to Steven's quick actions, starting CPR as fast as it was possible to start. I am so thankful to Steven Charie.

So, Dancing with the Stars (DWTS) saved my life. I would have been driving home had my wife not wanted to see it.

Steven Charie helped, too.

(When our families met, my oldest daughter Amanda told Steven's young daughter that her dad was a hero because he had saved my life. Steven's daughter's response: "My dad has always been my hero.")

I stayed at Evergreen in the Critical Care Unit for one day, and then transferred to Overlake Hospital which is in my "network." Pretty much all the tests that were run at Evergreen were repeated at Overlake, with the same results. The good news is that I had no blockages, no cholesterol, no gunk, no damage due to oxygen deprivation. The "Sudden Death Event" appeared to be caused by exercising for nearly an hour at a high level, which meant my heart was trying to pump a lot of blood through a pig valve that was too small. As a result, excessive pressure built up on one side of the pig valve until my heart said no more. The too-small pig valve was the problem and needed to be replaced. Don't trust pigs.

At Overlake, one of the surgeons was a heart valve specialist. He said he does more heart valve operations himself annually (250) than some entire cities. He was the logical choice. The good news is that the choice between the pig valve and the mechanical valve had changed in the past 11 years. There was a new mechanical valve that was still permanent, but required a much smaller dose of blood thinners such that I could still play soccer, hike, jog, etc. This new valve also allowed for a larger flow for the same size opening, making it effectively a 30% larger valve than the original pig valve using the same location. This new mechanical valve seemed like the obvious choice. The one decision I needed to make was that the surgeon was going to a two-week conference and if I had the surgery done before he left, it would be a second surgery, starting at 4:30 pm and extending until midnight or so, working with a tired staff. Otherwise, I would have to wait almost three weeks until he returned. I decided to wait and have a fresh staff operate.

The surgeon told me later that two of the sessions at his conference involved the general topic of how it was standard practice as little as ten years ago to put in heart valves that they now know to be too small.

I had another choice to make this time. Even though my problem had been identified as a too-small pig valve and that problem was fixed by the new mechanical valve, the fact was that my heart had had a "Sudden Death Event" which could make me more likely to have another one. As a result, we decided to have a second, more minor surgery to implant a defibrillator. This device would monitor my heart at all times and deliver a shock if my heart ever stopped again. The battery would last about ten years, so I would need a new battery once per decade. The only device like this is also a pacemaker. So, even though I do not need a pacemaker, I have one. If my heart ever needs to be "paced," the machine would just kick in automatically, and I would never know.

I know I would not know if it was turned on because at my first checkup I found out the pacemaker part had been accidently turned on and I had not known. They then turned it off and I could not tell.

Doctor count: I am still in contact with my original cardiologist from the pig valve days, now retired (1). I was assigned a cardiologist at Evergreen (2), then another at Overlake (3), because my regular cardiologist (4) was out of town at the time, but I was also assigned a cardiologist who specializes in implanted defibrillators (5). One Sunday at Overlake they were all gone, so I was assigned yet another cardiologist for just that day (6), and my current cardiologist reviewed my data with the woman who "wrote the book on Cardiology" due to the unusual situation (7). Additionally there was the surgeon (8) and I thought it wise to get a second, er, additional opinion from another heart-specialist surgeon (9). I was told to also see my plain, old regular doctor (10).

So that is where I am now. In theory, ready for soccer, jogging, hiking. As cardiologist #3 said, "no more than 139 floors on the Stairmaster."

I nearly died #8. Or did. Like a cat, I guess I have nine lives. So far.

But since I did a full "Restart" maybe I get a reset with nine new lives.

I can hope.

Mrs. Charie, Lisa, Tessa, Doug, Steven, Carolyn, Amanda, Lorraine and Steven's kids.

911 Dispatch—After my "death" I briefly did some training on 911 Dispatch, listening to many calls. The folks who answer those calls don't get enough credit! They save lives by talking folks through things like CPR, childbirth and sometimes both! They get help where needed quickly. They are the first first-responders.

I found a database that stored info about the call for me. The EMT unit arrived in less than four minutes. Again, I was awake and watched them arrive, thanks to Mr. Charie.

Most calls I listened to were sobering, but there were a few humorous moments:

One call reported an "umbrella fight" at a fast food restaurant. Then someone pulled a knife. The drive-through line of cars blocked the entrance, so the six stopped police cars with lights and sirens trying to get to the fight looked as though they were all in a hurry for take-out food. No one ended up getting hurt, but someone commented that you should not bring an umbrella to a knife fight.

Another time a drunk man called to say his friend was not breathing. Immediately, this triggers the dispatcher to give CPR instructions, which start with telling the caller to get the victim to lie on the floor. "Hey, Larry, lie down on the floor, we are going to start CPR on you," was heard in the background. If possible try to have someone who is not drunk call 911.

One woman called to report that "light, wispy smoke" was coming from her neighbor's chimney. She was thanked for her call.

One day multiple people called to report a naked woman walking down a main street. The first callers described her as about 30 years old. *Way more* officers than usual responded.

Ticking—I tick. That is, my heart valve does, faintly. My daughters can hear it and I don't think they like it. Fortunately, I cannot hear it. Usually. I would not be a good choice to join a bomb squad now. Or even to walk up behind one of the squad members. You would think walking through a security checkpoint while ticking would be a bad thing, but I get to go around metal detectors and it usually takes less time to get a pat-down than to go through the line.

This is my tick talk.

Questions From a Third Grader—An inquisitive third-grade student may make you realize the world has changed while you were not looking: What is a hubcap? Do you listen to "oldies rap"? What is a stamp? How did you learn things before the internet? What is a DVD? Why do they call it "rolling up" a window?

Tuesday Night Sports—The TV news always gives the same amount of time to sports on Tuesday night when there is no game.

Typical story: "Famous sports star signs autographs" or "broken bone will cause young sports star to miss two practices but not next game."

Unintentional Humor—In a certain insurance company's medical payments policy rider, the policy will pay medical costs for a person injured in the policy owner's home including medically necessary devices prescribed by a doctor EXCEPT if the doctor prescribes hot tubs, waterbeds or "anything that vibrates."

Unappreciated Humor—I went to the doctor to get a physical therapy (PT) referral for a minor hip issue. The doctor suggested Jon, who specializes in PT hip exercises. Me: "Is Jon a hippie?" The doctor, confused: "I don't think so..."

POOR BEDTIME STORIES FOR YOUNGSTERS

I put all the poor bedtime stories here in case someone wanted to tear out these pages (or erase them) so that you can leave this book for children to read. Or leave it in a school.

Huey's Mom—[Note: not a good bedtime story] I became friends with a guy named Huey in second grade. Huey didn't have a dad. Huey's mom took Huey and me to the YMCA one day. It was the first time I had ever been to a YMCA and I had a good time. I enjoyed telling Huey's mom all the fun things we did on the way back from the YMCA. Huey and I made plans to go again in a few weeks. But a few days later, Huey was gone and I never saw him again. I heard that Huey's mom had killed herself with a shotgun in her mouth. Huey had found her, and Huey was immediately taken to live with relatives in California.

Ben and Jay—[Note: not a good bedtime story] My first college roommate Jay was a born politician. He talked to everyone as though he had known them for years. He would walk up to you, and ask, "How have you been you F—er?" He called everyone a F—er and made it sound like a term of endearment.

Jay actually ran for the state legislature while in college. Although he lost the first time he ran, he was elected after college.

Anyway Jay had a way of making everyone feel comfortable and he would quickly get anyone he talked with to relax and smile. He could make friends with anyone.

Meanwhile, Ben was very shy. Ben tried to stay in his dorm room so as not to meet anyone. Ben's roommate realized that Ben needed some help making friends, so he got a bunch of us in the dorm to help. We wanted Ben to know there were a lot of folks on his side. We all had Ben watch Jay make friends with three people, one at a time.

Now, it was Ben's turn. Don't worry, we told him, we are on your side right here. Some random guy started walking toward us. OK, Ben make friends with this guy.

Ben stepped up to our unsuspecting random guy and stopped him. Ben looked at us. We were all right there, silently rooting for him. Ben turned back and we could see him start to twitch. His hands and arms started shaking a lot. He started to get red and hold his breath.

The guy was still there, wondering why Ben had stopped him.

Suddenly Ben screamed, "YOU F—ER!!!!!" at this poor guy.

Ben's roommate quickly rescued random guy, telling him not to worry, Ben was a great person, you'll like him once you get to know him, etc.

The rest of us were rolling on the floor laughing. Literally.

Breast Not Mentioned—[Note: Not a good bedtime story] I was at a pool one day when I saw that one of my teenage daughters' best friends was unaware that she had bounced out of the top of her swimsuit. I chose to pretend I didn't see it. Is there is a good way for the father of a teenage daughter to tell one of her daughter's best friends that her boob is hanging out?

Mansion Photos—[Note: not a good bedtime story] We often traded houses when we went on vacation. This worked well for us, as we have four children and vacations can be expensive as we often needed more than one hotel room. One year we traded our simple two-story house in the Seattle suburbs for a beautiful, five-story mansion in Brookline, a suburb of Boston. That Brookline neighborhood was full of mansions. We tried to introduce ourselves, and one by one each of the neighbors invited us in to see their classy homes. We saw one of the original homes in the Boston area—elegant with many amazing pieces of art. Another was owned by an inventor, with all sorts of fun inventions they didn't mind us photographing. These neighbors were nice folks, too. One woman invited us for lunch, and it was great.

The neighbors directly across the street had a very interesting house that was all black and looked somewhat like a castle. I especially wanted to tour it. I crossed the street and the two neighbors who seemed to live there were in the yard, gardening. They looked to be both in their late 50s and I assumed they were married. The man suggested that we come by on Tuesday at 7 pm to tour the house. Would we still be around? Yes, this was Sunday and we planned to stay past Tuesday, so that would be fine.

I arranged our day on Tuesday so that I would be ready to tour that home at 7 pm. I got our large 35mm camera with the big zoom lens and our large flash ready to go. I wanted the big flash so that I could take photos if it was dark. I had an extra camera as well for wide-angle shots. I knew the cameras and flash I had were big and bulky, but I wanted to get good photos. At exactly 7 pm, I crossed the street carrying my big cameras, flash plus my camera equipment bag over my shoulder. I climbed the front porch. The oversize door was wide open, but the screen door closed. It was about 80 degrees, so this made sense. As I raised my hand to knock on the screen door, I heard and saw the man I had seen earlier, um, let's say doing something in a Missionary Position on the sofa with a woman who looked to be about 20 years old. And there I was with my huge cameras, flash and camera bag like Mr. Paparazzi.

Good thing they were preoccupied.

Glad I didn't knock. I chose to quietly go back down the steps. I never did tour that house.

$85 Diet Coke—[Note: Not a good bedtime story] I was at the Las Vegas soccer tournament with the Shamrocks men's soccer team one year when I made plans with my friend Steve to meet in downtown Vegas. Downtown is about five miles from The Strip. Steve couldn't remember the name of the place where we were to meet, so he gave me directions (turn right, then left, then right, etc.). I got confused and I didn't have Steve's cell number. I don't like to be late when I am meeting someone, so I was getting concerned. I finally decided it must be one of two small casinos downtown where we were to meet. I walked into the first one, and was looking around for Steve. Two topless, and rather plain-looking (to be honest) women came up to me and asked if they could help me find someone. (Sure they were topless, but this was Vegas and they were wandering around the casino like it was normal). I said I was looking for Steve. They said they would help me find Steve, so I followed them. They asked me to sit in a chair and I was going to refuse because I was looking for Steve, but then I saw that the chair was situated such that it had the best view of the small casino, so I sat. It was dark, but from the chair I could see all the patrons, and determined that Steve was not there. One woman then sat on my knee and asked me if I had found Steve. I said no and got up to leave to go to the next casino, and two bouncers stopped me saying I had not paid. Paid for what? The lap dance. What? It is $75 for the lap dance plus you have to buy a drink. I don't drink. These bouncers were pretty insistent. I ended up buying a Diet Coke for $10, plus the $75 lap dance, so my diet Coke ended up being $85. And I never found Steve.

Although I didn't find Steve I did find a couple of other Shamrocks and sat with them to "enjoy" my $85 Diet Coke. They were amazed that the first thing I did after all this was call Lorraine. With me, what happens in Vegas gets told to my wife and then published in a book!

This became something of a legendary story with the Shamrocks. There are actually four affiliated Shamrock men's soccer teams in different age brackets. I got plenty of grief from the team I was actually playing on but at least I was still "Doug." On the other three teams I was "That $85 Diet Coke Guy."

When I told some guys from one of the other teams that this was my first and only lap dance and I didn't get the slightest bit—shall we say—excited, they bought me a "real" lap dance. They took me to a place in Vegas that was pretty much only booze and lap dances. I left after my "real" lap dance around midnight, but one of the guys got a "free" ride home from the manager at 8 am the next morning. He maxed out his credit cards buying lap dances and booze and didn't have enough money to buy a cab back to his luckily pre-paid hotel room.

No F-word—[Note: Not a good bedtime story] Jason was a guy on my men's soccer team when I was in my mid-20s. I remember Jason got injured in a game one day. He was on the ground and very upset, but over 90% of what he said was the F-word as adjective, noun, verb, you name it. No one could figure out what he was trying to say. He went on for about five minutes getting louder and louder, increasing to 99% f-word. Finally someone said, "Tell us what happened without using the F-word." Jason took a deep breath, and after a long pause, he said, "....he...pushed...me." The entire team started laughing, and Jason started up with the F-word again, now directed at us.

Jason was quite good looking and usually had a very cute woman watching him at our games but never the same one. One day we were carpooling to a game, just Jason and me. I asked Jason about the women he was dating. Jason told me that whenever he dated a woman, he tried everything he could think of, every line, so to speak, to get her to sleep with him on the first few dates. If she did, he never saw her again. Jason said he would never want a long-term relationship with a woman who would sleep with a guy after only a few dates.

Murdering Neighbors—[Note: Not a good bedtime story] Note the plural—*neighbors*. Due to an abundance of caution, I am going to call the two boys who lived across the street from us when we moved to Kirkland "X" and "Y." They were about five and two years old at the time we moved in. After watching five-year-old X for a couple of weeks, I remember turning to my wife and predicting that X would spend his entire adult life in prison. I was right. I could have made the same prediction about little brother Y as well.

X and Y were actually the grandsons of the woman who lived across the street from us. She was nice. She had two nice sons and a daughter who made poor choices with men. Daughter's first husband, the father of X and Y we were told was in prison in Alaska. She and her current boyfriend, a former police officer (pretty sure he was fired), kept having to move in with her mother, the boys' grandmother, for several weeks at a time, due to, um, housing issues.

The good news is that X and Y were only our neighbors for about two weeks every three or four years. When they were our temporary neighbors, they would do awful things in the neighborhood. I witnessed X knock a neighbor girl off her bike for no reason at all. I saw X throw rocks at kids he didn't know. X and Y would find dogs that were inside a home when the owners were gone, then go up to the window and see if they could get the dog to thrash and bark enough to knock over things and shred the curtains. They stole guns and liquor from another neighbor's house. You get the idea.

We don't have guns and liquor to steal, plus we get most of our stuff from garage sales. That is probably why they didn't steal from us.

The local police knew these two well. They had such a distinctive gait, the police would probably recognize them walking in a Halloween costume.

One day they were back in grandma's basement, and I saw a neighbor girl crying. I asked why. She said her bike was stolen, and it looked like a bike in grandma's yard, but she could not be sure and was afraid to enter the yard. I asked how she could identify her bike. She told me what to look for. I went into the yard to look for the identifying marks on the bike. While I was looking the boyfriend came outside and asked me what I was doing. I told him. He picked me up and threw me down the front stairs to the driveway. I am not a small guy—I am 6 foot 1 inch and I weigh over 250 pounds. I fell to the driveway. Although I was not hurt much, I immediately called 911. The responding officer told me that he knew this guy and his entire family well and they were scheduled to move to Florida in four days. He said if I pressed charges, that move would be delayed. The officer told me he would show up on the move day, and if they did not move, I could press assault charges. I could tell he wanted them in Florida as much as I did. The family moved to Florida on the scheduled day and I did not press charges.

A few years later, they moved back, fortunately not to grandma's basement, but unfortunately nearby. A few months after that, the boyfriend shot and killed the mother of X and Y. He shot her between the eyes with his gun. He claimed he was "cleaning his gun" and the "dog jumped" and caused the gun to fire. He said it was a coincidence that the bullet hit her between the eyes from close range. Since there had been multiple 911 calls for domestic violence in the previous weeks leading up to this no jury would have bought his story except for one thing—her son X testified in favor of his mother's killer.

Let's just say I cannot think of another person on earth who would testify in favor of his mother's killer.

The boyfriend was out of prison in less than a year thanks to X's testimony and almost immediately married another woman. I do not know if that woman is still alive. Hope so.

I am not sure who raised X and Y—both in their teens—after mom was dead and dad and mom's boyfriend were both in prison. But I do know that X was convicted as a teen of the murder of a girl in Kirkland.

This murder was complicated. X and a friend, let's call him J, were hired by a woman to kill her husband. They waited to ambush the husband coming home from work through the normal door but he chose to enter his house through a different door that day, and they got cold feet and decided to wait. Meanwhile, a daughter found out about the planned murder of her dad by her mom's co-conspirators and said she planned to go to authorities. It was this girl that X and J killed, to cover up their planned murder-for-hire. X got a sentence of 29 years for this murder.

His brother Y, meanwhile, ended up in prison as well, but for something other than murder. I was told a few years later that Y set a state record for getting charged with a felony less than 72 hours after being released from prison.

Horrifyingly, both brothers somehow separately escaped from separate prisons at about the same time. Fortunately, both went to Kirkland, where the police knew them well and they were caught quite quickly. As of this writing, both are back in prison, but neither has a life sentence.

After her two grandsons X and Y had been in prison for a few years, grandma decided to sell her house and move. We told the people who bought her house across the street from us, "We don't know who you are, but we love you!"

So, two murderers briefly lived across the street from us, and one of them assaulted me. One of many reasons I am lucky to be alive today.

I nearly died #6.

Lice—[Note: Not a good bedtime story] Lice are little insects that live on a person's short hairs, and prefer warm, dark places where they can drink blood. Hey ladies, can you think of a place like that?

Some say 2% of people world-wide have lice in their pubic region. Others say the percentage is much higher, as it is "under-reported."

I'll bet women in Brazil don't have lice.

Thank you for reading. Please tell your friends if you liked it, but not if you didn't.